3-Year Naturalization by Marriage to a U.S. Citizen

Getting US Citizenship through Marriage

Attorney Brian D. Lerner

LAW OFFICES OF
BRIAN D. LERNER
A PROFESSIONAL CORPORATION

ATTORNEY DRAFTED IMMIGRATION PETITIONS

By

Brian D. Lerner

Attorney at Law

Disclaimer and Terms of Use:

INTRODUCTION

There are a multitude of different immigration petitions and applications. They are complex and full of requirements. Obviously, it would be best to hire an immigration attorney to best prepare the petitions and applications. However, this can certainly cost thousands of dollars.

The next best option is to get a sample of the petition written by an experienced immigration attorney. The samples cost a fraction what would be charged by an immigration attorney. However, while the reader has to alter, amend and change the parts of the sample petition to reflect their actual situation, it is a fantastic roadmap for them to use. If the reader has purchased the entire petition or application, they will have real live samples of cover letters, forms, declarations, affidavits and the necessary exhibits to use. The samples come from real cases and the names of those clients have been redacted to protect the privacy of that person or corporation.

These are petitions and applications that have been drafted by an experienced immigration attorney with over 25 years of experience. Get the benefits of that experience without the costs.

CONTENTS

About the Law Offices of Brian D. Lerner

The Law Offices of Brian D. Lerner, APC. The law practice consists of Immigration and Nationality Law and everything involved with and regarding immigration which includes citizenhsip, investment visas, family and employment visas, removal and deportation hearings, appeals, waivers, adjustment, consulate processing and all types of immigration and citizenship matters. Thousands of families have been reunited and/or permitted to stay in the U.S. and/or return to the U.S. because of the successful work of Immigration Attorney Brian D. Lerner.

This law offices handles all types of immigration cases including family based and employment based. Immigration issues range from immigration court proceedings to trying to fix what paralegals may have done that was neither correct nor proper. Foreign nationals must have experience lawyers admitted to practice law.

The Law Offices of Brian D. Lerner, APC, handles cases arising from business visas, work permits, Green Cards, non-immigrant visas, deportation, citizenship, appeals and all areas of immigration. The Law Offices of Brian D. Lerner, APC does EB-5 Investor Visas, H-1B Specialty Occupation, L-1 Intracompany Transferee, E-2 Treaty Investor, E-1 Treaty Trader, O-1 Extraordinary Ability among others. Regarding immigrant visas for the Green Card, the firm does PERM and advanced degree PERM, Family Petitions, and Extraordinary Alien Petitions. In addition to affirmative petitions, the Law Firm represents people in people in deportation and removal hearings, including political asylum, withholding of removal, and convention against torture cases.

Brian D. Lerner has been certified as an expert in Immigration & Nationality Law by the California State Bar, Board of Legal Specialization since 2000 and has been re-certified three times. He now passes on his decades of experience by allowing the Reader, Law Schools, Professors and other Immigration Attorneys to purchase sample petitions on every facet of Immigration   Law.

About the Naturalization Application for a Lawful Permanent Resident Spouse who has been married to a United States Citizen Spouse for at least 3 years

The Spouse of a United States citizen who resides in the United States may be eligible for naturalization on the basis of his or her marriage. The spouse must have continuously resided in the United States after becoming a Lawful Permanent Resident for at least 3 years. The spouse must have lived in marital union with his or her United States citizen spouse for at least 3 years.

Law Offices of Brian D. Lerner

A PROFESSIONAL CORPORATION

CERTIFIED SPECIALIST IN IMMIGRATION AND NATIONALITY LAW
ADMITTED TO THE U.S. SUPREME COURT

LONG BEACH, CALIFORNIA
(562) 495-0154

September 18, 2020

U.S. Citizenship and Immigration Services
Attn: N-400
1820 E. Skyharbor Circle S, Suite 100
Phoenix, AZ 85034

Re: **N-400, Application for Naturalization**
        Applicant: Hussein Mukhtar Ta her ADBULHUSAIN
        Alien Number: 065-803-922

Dear Officer:

We hereby enclose the following in support of Applicant's N-400, Application for Naturalization:

Form: **Description:**

G-28   Notice of Entry of Appearance as Attorney or Accredited Representative; and
N-400   Application for Naturalization and $725.00 Filing Fee.

Table of Exhibits

Exhibit: **Description:**

1.   Applicant's Permanent Resident Card;
2.   Applicant's Passport;
3.   Applicant's Marriage Certificate;
4.   Applicant's Spouse's Naturalization Certificate;
5.   Applicant's Son's Birth Certificate; and
6.   Applicant's Joint 2018-2019 Income Tax Returns and W-2s

In the present case, Applicant is statutorily eligible for naturalization because he is at least 18-years-old, he is married to a U.S. citizen and lives in marital union with his spouse, he has been a lawful permanent resident for at least three (3) years, he has been physically present in the United States and resided in California for the requisite period prior to the filing of his application and, he has been a person of good moral character throughout the statutory period. *See* INA § 310 *et seq.*; INA §§ 316 and 319; 8 C.F.R. § 319.1.

//
//
//

Based on the foregoing, we respectfully request that the instant application be approved. If you should have any questions, please feel free to contact our office at (562) 495-0554.

Sincerely,

Christopher A. Reed
Attorney at Law

FORMS

**Notice of Entry of Appearance
as Attorney or Accredited Representative**

Department of Homeland Security

DHS
Form G-28
OMB No. 1615-0105
Expires 05/31/2021

Part 1. Information About Attorney or Accredited Representative

1. USCIS Online Account Number (if any)

   ▶

Name of Attorney or Accredited Representative

2.a. Family Name (Last Name) **Reed**

2.b. Given Name (First Name) **Christopher**

2.c. Middle Name **Allan**

Address of Attorney or Accredited Representative

3.a. Street Number and Name **3233 E. Broadway**

3.b. ☐ Apt. ☐ Ste. ☐ Flr.

3.c. City or Town **Long Beach**

3.d. State **CA**   3.e. ZIP Code **90803**

3.f. Province

3.g. Postal Code

3.h. Country

   USA

Contact Information of Attorney or Accredited Representative

4. Daytime Telephone Number

   (562) 495-0554

5. Mobile Telephone Number (if any)

   N/A

6. Email Address (if any)

   creed@eimmigration.org

7. Fax Number (if any)

   (562) 512-2038

Part 2. Eligibility Information for Attorney or Accredited Representative

Select all applicable items.

1.a. ☒ I am an attorney eligible to practice law in, and a member in good standing of, the bar of the highest courts of the following states, possessions, territories, commonwealths, or the District of Columbia. If you need extra space to complete this section, use the space provided in **Part 6. Additional Information**.

   Licensing Authority

   California Supreme Court

1.b. Bar Number (if applicable)

   235438

1.c. I (select only one box) ☒ am not ☐ am subject to any order suspending, enjoining, restraining, disbarring, or otherwise restricting me in the practice of law. If you are subject to any orders, use the space provided in **Part 6. Additional Information** to provide an explanation.

1.d. Name of Law Firm or Organization (if applicable)

   Law Offices of Brian D. Lerner, APC

2.a. ☐ I am an accredited representative of the following qualified nonprofit religious, charitable, social service, or similar organization established in the United States and recognized by the Department of Justice in accordance with 8 CFR part 1292.

2.b. Name of Recognized Organization

2.c. Date of Accreditation (mm/dd/yyyy)

3. ☐ I am associated with

   ,
   the attorney or accredited representative of record who previously filed Form G-28 in this case, and my appearance as an attorney or accredited representative for a limited purpose is at his or her request.

4.a. ☐ I am a law student or law graduate working under the direct supervision of the attorney or accredited representative of record on this form in accordance with the requirements in 8 CFR 292.1(a)(2).

4.b. Name of Law Student or Law Graduate

4488

Form G-28 09/17/18

Part 3. Notice of Appearance as Attorney or Accredited Representative

If you need extra space to complete this section, use the space provided in **Part 6. Additional Information.**

This appearance relates to immigration matters before (select **only one box**):

1.a. ☒ U.S. Citizenship and Immigration Services (USCIS)

1.b. List the form numbers or specific matter in which appearance is entered.

> N-400

2.a. ☐ U.S. Immigration and Customs Enforcement (ICE)

2.b. List the specific matter in which appearance is entered.

3.a. ☐ U.S. Customs and Border Protection (CBP)

3.b. List the specific matter in which appearance is entered.

4. Receipt Number (if any)

5. I enter my appearance as an attorney or accredited representative at the request of the (select **only one box**):

☒ Applicant ☐ Petitioner ☐ Requestor
☐ Beneficiary/Derivative ☐ Respondent (ICE, CBP)

Information About Client (Applicant, Petitioner, Requestor, Beneficiary or Derivative, Respondent, or Authorized Signatory for an Entity)

6.a. Family Name (Last Name) | **ABDULHUSAIN**

6.b. Given Name (First Name) | **Hussein**

6.c. Middle Name | **Mukhtar Taher**

7.a. Name of Entity (if applicable)

7.b. Title of Authorized Signatory for Entity (if applicable)

8. Client's USCIS Online Account Number (if any)

9. Client's Alien Registration Number (A-Number) (if any)

> ► A- | 0 6 5 8 0 3 9 2 2

Client's Contact Information

10. Daytime Telephone Number

> **(310) 999-4788**

11. Mobile Telephone Number (if any)

> **(310) 999-4788**

12. Email Address (if any)

> **hussainmukhtar@gmail.com**

Mailing Address of Client

NOTE: Provide the client's mailing address. **Do not** provide the business mailing address of the attorney or accredited representative **unless** it serves as the safe mailing address on the application or petition being filed with this Form G-28.

13.a. Street Number and Name | **730 S. Beach Boulevard**

13.b. ☒ Apt. ☐ Ste. ☐ Flr. | **28**

13.c. City or Town | **Anaheim**

13.d. State **CA** 13.e. ZIP Code **92804**

13.f. Province

13.g. Postal Code

13.h. Country

> **USA**

Part 4. Client's Consent to Representation and Signature

Consent to Representation and Release of Information

I have requested the representation of and consented to being represented by the attorney or accredited representative named in **Part 1.** of this form. According to the Privacy Act of 1974 and U.S. Department of Homeland Security (DHS) policy, I also consent to the disclosure to the named attorney or accredited representative of any records pertaining to me that appear in any system of records of USCIS, ICE, or CBP.

Part 4. Client's Consent to Representation and Signature (continued)

Options Regarding Receipt of USCIS Notices and Documents

USCIS will send notices to both a represented party (the client) and his, her, or its attorney or accredited representative either through mail or electronic delivery. USCIS will send all secure identity documents and Travel Documents to the client's U.S. mailing address.

If you want to have notices and/or secure identity documents sent to your attorney or accredited representative of record rather than to you, please select **all applicable** items below. You may change these elections through written notice to USCIS.

1.a. ☒ I request that USCIS send original notices on an application or petition to the business address of my attorney or accredited representative as listed in this form.

1.b. ☐ I request that USCIS send any secure identity document (Permanent Resident Card, Employment Authorization Document, or Travel Document) that I receive to the U.S. business address of my attorney or accredited representative (or to a designated military or diplomatic address in a foreign country (if permitted)).

   NOTE: If your notice contains Form I-94, Arrival-Departure Record, USCIS will send the notice to the U.S. business address of your attorney or accredited representative. If you would rather have your Form I-94 sent directly to you, select **Item Number 1.c.**

1.c. ☐ I request that USCIS send my notice containing Form I-94 to me at my U.S. mailing address.

Signature of Client or Authorized Signatory for an Entity

2.a. Signature of Client or Authorized Signatory for an Entity

➡

2.b. Date of Signature (mm/dd/yyyy)   09/16/2020

Part 5. Signature of Attorney or Accredited Representative

I have read and understand the regulations and conditions contained in 8 CFR 103.2 and 292 governing appearances and representation before DHS. I declare under penalty of perjury under the laws of the United States that the information I have provided on this form is true and correct.

1.a. Signature of Attorney or Accredited Representative

1.b. Date of Signature (mm/dd/yyyy)   09/16/2020

2.a. Signature of Law Student or Law Graduate

2.b. Date of Signature (mm/dd/yyyy)

Part 6. Additional Information

If you need extra space to provide any additional information within this form, use the space below. If you need more space than what is provided, you may make copies of this page to complete and file with this form or attach a separate sheet of paper. Type or print your name at the top of each sheet; indicate the **Page Number**, **Part Number**, and **Item Number** to which your answer refers; and sign and date each sheet.

1.a Family Name (Last Name): **ABDULHUSAIN**

1.b. Given Name (First Name): **Hussein**

1.c. Middle Name: **Mukhtar Taher**

2.a. Page Number

2.b. Part Number

2.c. Item Number

2.d.

3.a. Page Number

3.b. Part Number

3.c. Item Number

3.d.

4.a. Page Number

4.b. Part Number

4.c. Item Number

4.d.

5.a. Page Number

5.b. Part Number

5.c. Item Number

5.d.

6.a. Page Number

6.b. Part Number

6.c. Item Number

6.d.

Application for Naturalization

Department of Homeland Security
U.S. Citizenship and Immigration Services

For USCIS Use Only	Date Stamp	Receipt	Action Block
Remarks			

▶ **START HERE - Type or print in black ink.** Type or print "N/A" if an item is not applicable or the answer is none, unless otherwise indicated. Failure to answer all of the questions may delay U.S. Citizenship and Immigration Services (USCIS) processing your Form N-400. **NOTE: You must complete Parts 1. - 15.**

If your biological or legal adoptive mother or father is a U.S. citizen by birth, or was naturalized before you reached your 18th birthday, you may already be a U.S. citizen. Before you consider filing this application, please visit the USCIS Website at www.uscis.gov for more information on this topic and to review the instructions for Form N-600, Application for Certificate of Citizenship, and Form N-600K, Application for Citizenship and Issuance of Certificate Under Section 322.

NOTE: Are either of your parents a United States citizen? If you answer "Yes," then complete **Part 6. Information About Your Parents** as part of this application. If you answer "No," then skip **Part 6.** and go to **Part 7. Biographic Information.**

Part 1. Information About Your Eligibility (Select only one box or your Form N-400 may be delayed)

Enter Your 9 Digit A-Number:
▶ A- | 0 | 6 | 5 | 8 | 0 | 3 | 9 | 2 | 2 |

1. You are at least 18 years of age **and:**

   A. ☐ Have been a lawful permanent resident of the United States for at least 5 years.

   B. ☒ Have been a lawful permanent resident of the United States for at least 3 years. In addition, you have been married to and living with the same U.S. citizen spouse for the last 3 years, **and** your spouse has been a U.S. citizen for the last 3 years at the time you filed your Form N-400.

   C. ☐ Are a lawful permanent resident of the United States **and** you are the spouse of a U.S. citizen **and** your U.S. citizen spouse is regularly engaged in specified employment abroad. (See the Immigration and Nationality Act (INA) section 319(b).) If your residential address is outside the United States and you are filing under Section 319(b), select the USCIS Field Office from the list below where you would like to have your naturalization interview:

   [ ]

   D. ☐ Are applying on the basis of qualifying military service.

   E. ☐ Other (Explain):

Part 2. Information About You (Person applying for naturalization)

1. Your Current Legal Name (**do not** provide a nickname)

Family Name (Last Name)	Given Name (First Name)	Middle Name (if applicable)
ABDULHUSAIN	Hussein	Mukhtar Taher

2. Your Name Exactly As It Appears on Your Permanent Resident Card (if applicable)

Family Name (Last Name)	Given Name (First Name)	Middle Name (if applicable)
ABDULHUSAIN	Hussein	Mukhtar Ta

Part 2. Information About You (Person applying for naturalization) (continued)

3. Other Names You Have Used Since Birth (include nicknames, aliases, and maiden name, if applicable)

Family Name (Last Name)	Given Name (First Name)	Middle Name (if applicable)
N/A	N/A	N/A
N/A	N/A	N/A

4. Name Change (Optional)

Read the Form N-400 Instructions before you decide whether or not you would like to legally change your name.

Would you like to legally change your name? ☐ Yes ☒ No

If you answered "Yes," type or print the new name you would like to use in the spaces provided below.

Family Name (Last Name)	Given Name (First Name)	Middle Name (if applicable)

5. U.S. Social Security Number (if applicable) ► 6 1 7 7 5 5 6 7 9

6. USCIS Online Account Number (if any) ►

7. Gender ☒ Male ☐ Female

8. Date of Birth (mm/dd/yyyy) 08/10/1989

9. Date You Became a Lawful Permanent Resident (mm/dd/yyyy) 07/06/2017

10. Country of Birth Saudi Arabia

11. Country of Citizenship or Nationality Yemen

12. Do you have a physical or developmental disability or mental impairment that prevents you from demonstrating your knowledge and understanding of the English language and/or civics requirements for naturalization? ☐ Yes ☒ No

If you answered "Yes," submit a completed Form N-648, Medical Certification for Disability Exceptions, when you file your Form N-400.

13. Exemptions from the English Language Test

A. Are you **50** years of age or older **and** have you lived in the United States as a lawful permanent resident for periods totaling at least **20** years at the time you file your Form N-400? ☐ Yes ☐ No

B. Are you **55** years of age or older **and** have you lived in the United States as a lawful permanent resident for periods totaling at least **15** years at the time you file your Form N-400? ☐ Yes ☐ No

C. Are you **65** years of age or older **and** have you lived in the United States as a lawful permanent resident for periods totaling at least **20** years at the time you file your Form N-400? (If you meet this requirement, you will also be given a simplified version of the civics test.) ☐ Yes ☐ No

Part 3. Accommodations for Individuals With Disabilities and/or Impairments

NOTE: Read the information in the Form N-400 Instructions before completing this part.

1. Are you requesting an accommodation because of your disabilities and/or impairments? ☐ Yes ☒ No

If you answered "Yes," select any applicable box.

A. ☐ I am deaf or hard of hearing and request the following accommodation. (If you are requesting a sign-language interpreter, indicate for which language (for example, American Sign Language).)

B. ☐ I am blind or have low vision and request the following accommodation:

C. ☐ I have another type of disability and/or impairment (for example, use a wheelchair). (Describe the nature of your disability and/or impairment and the accommodation you are requesting.)

Part 4. Information to Contact You

1. Daytime Telephone Number

(310) 999-4788

2. Work Telephone Number (if any)

(310) 999-4788

3. Evening Telephone Number

(310) 999-4788

4. Mobile Telephone Number (if any)

(310) 999-4788

5. Email Address (if any)

hussainmukhtar@gmail.com

Part 5. Information About Your Residence

1. Where have you lived during the last five years? Provide your most recent residence and then list every location where you have lived during the last five years. If you need extra space, use additional sheets of paper.

A. Current Physical Address

Street Number and Name | Apt. | Ste. | Flr. | Number
730 S. Beach Boulevard | ☒ | ☐ | ☐ | 28

City or Town	County	State	ZIP Code + 4
Anaheim	Orange	CA	92804 -

Province or Region (foreign address only)	Postal Code (foreign address only)	Country (foreign address only)
N/A	N/A	USA

Dates of Residence | From (mm/dd/yyyy) 03/2019 | To (mm/dd/yyyy) Present

B. Current Mailing Address (if different from the address above)

In Care Of Name (if any)

N/A

Street Number and Name | Apt. | Ste. | Flr. | Number
730 S. Beach Boulevard | ☒ | ☐ | ☐ | 28

City or Town	County	State	ZIP Code + 4
Anaheim	Orange	CA	92804 -

Province or Region (foreign address only)	Postal Code (foreign address only)	Country (foreign address only)
N/A	N/A	USA

C. Physical Address 2

Street Number and Name   Apt. Ste. Flr. Number

2447 W. Orange Avenue   ☐ ☐ ☐

City or Town   County   State   ZIP Code + 4

Anaheim   Orange   CA   92804 -

Province or Region   Postal Code   Country
(foreign address only)   (foreign address only)   (foreign address only)

                                                    USA

Dates of   From (mm/dd/yyyy)   To (mm/dd/yyyy)
Residence   01/2017   03/2019

D. Physical Address 3

Street Number and Name   Apt. Ste. Flr. Number

N/A   ☐ ☐ ☐ N/A

City or Town   County   State   ZIP Code + 4

N/A   N/A   N/A   N/A -

Province or Region   Postal Code   Country
(foreign address only)   (foreign address only)   (foreign address only)

N/A   N/A   N/A

Dates of   From (mm/dd/yyyy)   To (mm/dd/yyyy)
Residence   N/A   N/A

E. Physical Address 4

Street Number and Name   Apt. Ste. Flr. Number

N/A   ☐ ☐ ☐ N/A

City or Town   County   State   ZIP Code + 4

N/A   N/A   N/A   N/A -

Province or Region   Postal Code   Country
(foreign address only)   (foreign address only)   (foreign address only)

N/A   N/A   N/A

Dates of   From (mm/dd/yyyy)   To (mm/dd/yyyy)
Residence   N/A   N/A

Part 6. Information About Your Parents

If neither one of your parents is a United States citizen, then skip this part and go to Part 7.

1. Were your parents married before your 18th birthday?   ☒ Yes ☐ No

Information About Your Mother

2. Is your mother a U.S. citizen?   ☐ Yes ☒ No

   If you answered "Yes," complete the following information. If you answered "No," go to Item Number 3.

| Part 6. Information About Your Parents (continued) | | A- | 0 | 6 | 5 | 8 | 0 | 3 | 9 | 2 | 2 |

A. Current Legal Name of U.S. Citizen Mother

Family Name (Last Name)	Given Name (First Name)	Middle Name (if applicable)

B. Mother's Country of Birth

C. Mother's Date of Birth (mm/dd/yyyy)

D. Date Mother Became a U.S. Citizen (if known) (mm/dd/yyyy)

E. Mother's A-Number (if any)

▶ A-

Information About Your Father

3. Is your father a U.S. citizen? ☐ Yes ☒ No

If you answered "Yes," complete the information below. If you answered "No," go to **Part 7.**

A. Current Legal Name of U.S. Citizen Father

Family Name (Last Name)	Given Name (First Name)	Middle Name (if applicable)

B. Father's Country of Birth

C. Father's Date of Birth (mm/dd/yyyy)

D. Date Father Became a U.S. Citizen (if known) (mm/dd/yyyy)

E. Father's A-Number (if any)

▶ A-

Part 7. Biographic Information

NOTE: USCIS requires you to complete the categories below to conduct background checks. (See the Form N-400 Instructions for more information.)

1. Ethnicity (Select **only one** box)

    ☐ Hispanic or Latino ☒ Not Hispanic or Latino

2. Race (Select **all applicable** boxes)

    ☒ White ☒ Asian ☐ Black or African American ☐ American Indian or Alaska Native ☐ Native Hawaiian or Other Pacific Islander

3. Height Feet **5** Inches **8** 4. Weight Pounds **1 5 0**

5. Eye color (Select **only one** box)

    ☐ Black ☐ Blue ☒ Brown ☐ Gray ☐ Green ☐ Hazel ☐ Maroon ☐ Pink ☐ Unknown/ Other

6. Hair color (Select **only one** box)

    ☐ Bald (No hair) ☒ Black ☐ Blond ☐ Brown ☐ Gray ☐ Red ☐ Sandy ☐ White ☐ Unknown/ Other

Part 8. Information About Your Employment and Schools You Attended | A- | 0 6 5 8 0 3 9 2 2

List where you have worked or attended school full time or part time during the last five years. Provide information for the complete time period. Include all military, police, and/or intelligence service. Begin by providing information about your most recent or current employment, studies, or unemployment (if applicable). Provide the locations and dates where you worked, were self-employed, were unemployed, or have studied for the last five years. If you worked for yourself, type or print "self-employed." If you were unemployed, type or print "unemployed." If you need extra space, use additional sheets of paper.

1. Employer or School Name

Instacart

Street Number and Name: 730 S. Beach Boulevard — Apt. ☒ Ste. ☐ Flr. ☐ Number 28

City or Town: Anaheim | State: CA | ZIP Code + 4: 92804 -

Province or Region (foreign address only): N/A | Postal Code (foreign address only): N/A | Country (foreign address only): N/A

Date From (mm/dd/yyyy): 08/2020 | Date To (mm/dd/yyyy): PRESENT | Your Occupation: Shopper

2. Employer or School Name

Al Khair Perfumery

Street Number and Name: 6613 Al Bukhariyah Lane — Apt. ☐ Ste. ☐ Flr. ☐ Number

City or Town: Jeddah | State: | ZIP Code + 4: -

Province or Region (foreign address only): N/A | Postal Code (foreign address only): 22233 | Country (foreign address only): Saudia Arabia

Date From (mm/dd/yyyy): 2012 | Date To (mm/dd/yyyy): PRESENT | Your Occupation: Financial Business Consultant

3. Employer or School Name

Uber/Lyft

Street Number and Name: 730 S. Beach Boulevard — Apt. ☒ Ste. ☐ Flr. ☐ Number 28

City or Town: Anaheim | State: CA | ZIP Code + 4: 92804 -

Province or Region (foreign address only): N/A | Postal Code (foreign address only): N/A | Country (foreign address only): N/A

Date From (mm/dd/yyyy): 02/2019 | Date To (mm/dd/yyyy): 03/2020 | Your Occupation: Driver

Part 9. Time Outside the United States

1. How many **total days (24 hours or longer)** did you spend outside the United States during the last 5 years? **504** days

2. How many trips of **24 hours or longer** have you taken outside the United States during the last 5 years? **5** trips

3. List below all the trips of **24 hours or longer** that you have taken outside the United States during the last 5 years. Start with your most recent trip and work backwards. If you need extra space, use additional sheets of paper.

Date You Left the United States (mm/dd/yyyy)	Date You Returned to the United States (mm/dd/yyyy)	Did Trip Last 6 Months or More?	Countries to Which You Traveled	Total Days Outside the United States
01/18/2020	02/26/2020	☐ Yes ☒ No	India, Saudi Arabia, Pakistan, Turkey	40
05/22/2019	06/19/2019	☐ Yes ☒ No	Saudi Arabia	29
07/14/2018	12/26/2018	☐ Yes ☒ No	Saudi Arabia, Turkey	166
01/23/2018	06/07/2018	☐ Yes ☒ No	Saudi Arabia, India, Pakistan,	136
08/08/2017	12/18/2017	☐ Yes ☒ No	India, UAE, Saudi Arabia, Turkey	133
		☐ Yes ☐ No		

Part 10. Information About Your Marital History

1. What is your current marital status?

   ☐ Single, Never Married ☒ Married ☐ Divorced ☐ Widowed ☐ Separated ☐ Marriage Annulled

   If you are single and have **never** married, go to **Part 11.**

2. If you are married, is your spouse a current member of the U.S. armed forces? ☐ Yes ☒ No

3. How many times have you been married (including annulled marriages, marriages to other people, and marriages to the same person)? **1**

4. If you are married now, provide the following information about your current spouse.

   A. Current Spouse's Legal Name

Family Name (Last Name)	Given Name (First Name)	Middle Name (if applicable)
ABDULHUSAIN	Sharish	Khandia

   B. Current Spouse's Previous Legal Name

Family Name (Last Name)	Given Name (First Name)	Middle Name (if applicable)
KHANDIA	Sharish	Belal

   C. Other Names Used by Current Spouse (include nicknames, aliases, and maiden name, if applicable)

Family Name (Last Name)	Given Name (First Name)	Middle Name (if applicable)
N/A	N/A	N/A

   D. Current Spouse's Date of Birth (mm/dd/yyyy)
   10/24/1987

   E. Date You Entered into Marriage with Current Spouse (mm/dd/yyyy)
   01/05/2016

Part 10. Information About Your Marital History (continued)   A- 0 6 5 8 0 3 9 2 2

    F. Current Spouse's Present Home Address

Street Number and Name | Apt. Ste. Flr. Number

730 S. Beach Boulevard   ☒ ☐ ☐ 28

City or Town: Anaheim

County: Orange

State: CA

ZIP Code + 4: 92804 -

Province or Region (foreign address only): N/A

Postal Code (foreign address only): N/A

Country (foreign address only): USA

    G. Current Spouse's Current Employer or Company

Instacart and Shipt (Self-Employed)

5. Is your current spouse a U.S. citizen?   ☒ Yes ☐ No

If you answered "Yes," answer **Item Number 6.** If you answered "No," go to **Item Number 7.**

6. If your current spouse is a U.S. citizen, complete the following information.

    A. When did your current spouse become a U.S. citizen?

      ☐ At Birth - Go to **Item Number 8.**   ☒ Other - Complete the following information.

    B. Date Your Current Spouse Became a U.S. Citizen (mm/dd/yyyy)

    03/18/2015

7. If your current spouse is not a U.S. citizen, complete the following information.

    A. Current Spouse's Country of Citizenship or Nationality

    B. Current Spouse's A-Number (if any)   ▶ A-

    C. Current Spouse's Immigration Status

      ☐ Lawful Permanent Resident   ☐ Other (Explain):

8. How many times has your current spouse been married (including annulled marriages, marriages to other people, and marriages to the same person)? If your current spouse has been married before, provide the following information about your current spouse's prior spouse.   1

If your current spouse has had more than one previous marriage, provide that information on additional sheets of paper.

    A. Legal Name of My Current Spouse's Prior Spouse

Family Name (Last Name): N/A

Given Name (First Name): N/A

Middle Name (if applicable): N/A

    B. Immigration Status of My Current Spouse's Prior Spouse (if known)

      ☐ U.S. Citizen   ☐ Lawful Permanent Resident   ☐ Other (Explain):

    C. Date of Birth of My Current Spouse's Prior Spouse (mm/dd/yyyy): N/A

    D. Country of Birth of My Current Spouse's Prior Spouse: N/A

    E. Country of Citizenship or Nationality of My Current Spouse's Prior Spouse: N/A

Part 10. Information About Your Marital History (continued)	A-	0 6 5 8 0 3 9 2 2

F. My Current Spouse's Date of Marriage with Prior Spouse (mm/dd/yyyy)

N/A

G. Date My Current Spouse's Marriage Ended with Prior Spouse (mm/dd/yyyy)

N/A

H. How My Current Spouse's Marriage Ended with Prior Spouse

☐ Annulled ☐ Divorced ☐ Spouse Deceased ☐ Other (Explain):

9. If you were married before, provide the following information about your prior spouse. If you have more than one previous marriage, provide that information on additional sheets of paper.

A. My Prior Spouse's Legal Name

Family Name (Last Name)	Given Name (First Name)	Middle Name (if applicable)
N/A	N/A	N/A

B. My Prior Spouse's Immigration Status When My Marriage Ended (if known)

☐ U.S. Citizen ☐ Lawful Permanent Resident ☐ Other (Explain):

C. My Prior Spouse's Date of Birth (mm/dd/yyyy)

N/A

D. My Prior Spouse's Country of Birth

N/A

E. My Prior Spouse's Country of Citizenship or Nationality

N/A

F. Date of Marriage with My Prior Spouse (mm/dd/yyyy)

N/A

G. Date Marriage Ended with My Prior Spouse (mm/dd/yyyy)

N/A

H. How Marriage Ended with My Prior Spouse

☐ Annulled ☐ Divorced ☐ Spouse Deceased ☐ Other (Explain):

Part 11. Information About Your Children

1. Indicate your total number of children. (You must indicate ALL children, including: children who are alive, missing, or deceased; children born in the United States or in other countries; children under 18 years of age or older; children who are currently married or unmarried; children living with you or elsewhere; current stepchildren; legally adopted children; **and** children born when you were not married.)

1

2. Provide the following information about all your children (sons and daughters) listed in **Item Number 1.**, regardless of age. To list any additional children, use additional sheets of paper.

A. Child 1

Current Legal Name

Family Name (Last Name)	Given Name (First Name)	Middle Name (if applicable)
N/A	N/A	N/A

A-Number (if any)

► A- N/A

Date of Birth (mm/dd/yyyy)

N/A

Country of Birth

N/A

 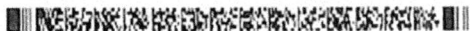

Part 11. Information About Your Children (continued)   A- | 0 | 6 | 5 | 8 | 0 | 3 | 9 | 2 | 2 |

Current Address

Street Number and Name

N/A   Apt. ☐ Ste. ☐ Flr. ☐ Number N/A

City or Town	County	State	ZIP Code + 4
N/A	N/A	N/A	N/A -

Province or Region (foreign address only) — N|A

Postal Code (foreign address only) — N|A

Country (foreign address only) — N/A

What is your child's relationship to you? (for example, biological child, stepchild, legally adopted child)   N/A

B. Child 2

Current Legal Name

Family Name (Last Name)	Given Name (First Name)	Middle Name (if applicable)
N/A	N/A	N/A

A-Number (if any) ► A- N|A

Date of Birth (mm/dd/yyyy) N/A

Country of Birth N/A

Current Address

Street Number and Name

N/A   Apt. ☐ Ste. ☐ Flr. ☐ Number N/A

City or Town	County	State	ZIP Code + 4
N/A	N/A	N/A	N/A -

Province or Region (foreign address only)

Postal Code (foreign address only)

Country (foreign address only) — N/A

What is your child's relationship to you? (for example, biological child, stepchild, legally adopted child)   N/A

C. Child 3

Current Legal Name

Family Name (Last Name)	Given Name (First Name)	Middle Name (if applicable)
N/A	N/A	N/A

A-Number (if any) ► A- N|A

Date of Birth (mm/dd/yyyy) N/A

Country of Birth N/A

 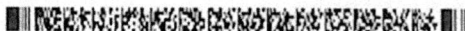

| Part 11. Information About Your Children (continued) | | A- 0 6 5 8 0 3 9 2 2 |

Current Address

Street Number and Name · Apt. Ste. Flr. Number

N/A · ☐ ☐ ☐ N/A

| City or Town | County | State | ZIP Code + 4 |
| N/A | N/A | N/A | N/A - |

| Province or Region (foreign address only) | Postal Code (foreign address only) | Country (foreign address only) |
| N/A | N/A | N/A |

What is your child's relationship to you? (for example, biological child, stepchild, legally adopted child) · N/A

D. Child 4

Current Legal Name

| Family Name (Last Name) | Given Name (First Name) | Middle Name (if applicable) |
| ABDULHUSAIN | Ayaan | Hussein |

| A-Number (if any) | Date of Birth (mm/dd/yyyy) | Country of Birth |
| ▶ A- N/A | 04/05/2019 | USA |

Current Address

Street Number and Name · Apt. Ste. Flr. Number

730 S. Beach Boulevard · ☒ ☐ ☐ 28

| City or Town | County | State | ZIP Code + 4 |
| Anaheim | Orange | CA | 92804 - |

| Province or Region (foreign address only) | Postal Code (foreign address only) | Country (foreign address only) |
| N/A | N/A | USA |

What is your child's relationship to you? (for example, biological child, stepchild, legally adopted child) · Biological Child

Part 12. Additional Information About You (Person Applying for Naturalization)

Answer Item Numbers 1. - 21. If you answer "Yes" to any of these questions, include a typed or printed explanation on additional sheets of paper.

1. Have you EVER claimed to be a U.S. citizen (in writing or any other way)? ☐ Yes ☒ No

2. Have you EVER registered to vote in any Federal, state, or local election in the United States? ☐ Yes ☒ No

3. Have you EVER voted in any Federal, state, or local election in the United States? ☐ Yes ☒ No

4. A. Do you now have, or did you EVER have, a hereditary title or an order of nobility in any foreign country? ☐ Yes ☒ No

   B. If you answered "Yes," are you willing to give up any inherited titles or orders of nobility that you have in a foreign country at your naturalization ceremony? ☐ Yes ☐ No

5. Have you EVER been declared legally incompetent or been confined to a mental institution? ☐ Yes ☒ No

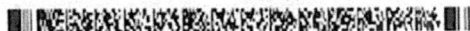

6. Do you owe any overdue Federal, state, or local taxes? ☐ Yes ☒ No

7. A. Have you **EVER** not filed a Federal, state, or local tax return since you became a lawful permanent resident? ☐ Yes ☒ No

 B. If you answered "Yes," did you consider yourself to be a "non-U.S. resident"? ☐ Yes ☐ No

8. Have you called yourself a "non-U.S. resident" on a Federal, state, or local tax return since you became a lawful permanent resident? ☐ Yes ☒ No

9. A. Have you **EVER** been a member of, involved in, or in any way associated with, any organization, association, fund, foundation, party, club, society, or similar group in the United States or in any other location in the world? ☐ Yes ☒ No

 B. If you answered "Yes," provide the information below. If you need extra space, attach the names of the other groups on additional sheets of paper and provide any evidence to support your answers.

Name of the Group	Purpose of the Group	Dates of Membership	
		From (mm/dd/yyyy)	To (mm/dd/yyyy)

10. Have you **EVER** been a member of, or in any way associated (either directly or indirectly) with:

 A. The Communist Party? ☐ Yes ☒ No

 B. Any other totalitarian party? ☐ Yes ☒ No

 C. A terrorist organization? ☐ Yes ☒ No

11. Have you **EVER** advocated (either directly or indirectly) the overthrow of any government by force or violence? ☐ Yes ☒ No

12. Have you **EVER** persecuted (either directly or indirectly) any person because of race, religion, national origin, membership in a particular social group, or political opinion? ☐ Yes ☒ No

13. Between March 23, 1933 and May 8, 1945, did you work for or associate in any way (either directly or indirectly) with:

 A. The Nazi government of Germany? ☐ Yes ☒ No

 B. Any government in any area occupied by, allied with, or established with the help of the Nazi government of Germany? ☐ Yes ☒ No

 C. Any German, Nazi, or S.S. military unit, paramilitary unit, self-defense unit, vigilante unit, citizen unit, police unit, government agency or office, extermination camp, concentration camp, prisoner of war camp, prison, labor camp, or transit camp? ☐ Yes ☒ No

Part 12. **Additional Information About You** (Person Applying for Naturalization) (continued)

14. Were you **EVER** involved in any way with any of the following:

    A. Genocide? ☐ Yes ☒ No

    B. Torture? ☐ Yes ☒ No

    C. Killing, or trying to kill, someone? ☐ Yes ☒ No

    D. Badly hurting, or trying to hurt, a person on purpose? ☐ Yes ☒ No

    E. Forcing, or trying to force, someone to have any kind of sexual contact or relations? ☐ Yes ☒ No

    F. Not letting someone practice his or her religion? ☐ Yes ☒ No

15. Were you **EVER** a member of, or did you **EVER** serve in, help, or otherwise participate in, any of the following groups:

    A. Military unit? ☐ Yes ☒ No

    B. Paramilitary unit (a group of people who act like a military group but are not part of the official military)? ☐ Yes ☒ No

    C. Police unit? ☐ Yes ☒ No

    D. Self-defense unit? ☐ Yes ☒ No

    E. Vigilante unit (a group of people who act like the police, but are not part of the official police)? ☐ Yes ☒ No

    F. Rebel group? ☐ Yes ☒ No

    G. Guerrilla group (a group of people who use weapons against or otherwise physically attack the military, police, government, or other people)? ☐ Yes ☒ No

    H. Militia (an army of people, not part of the official military)? ☐ Yes ☒ No

    I. Insurgent organization (a group that uses weapons and fights against a government)? ☐ Yes ☒ No

16. Were you **EVER** a worker, volunteer, or soldier, or did you otherwise **EVER** serve in any of the following:

    A. Prison or jail? ☐ Yes ☒ No

    B. Prison camp? ☐ Yes ☒ No

    C. Detention facility (a place where people are forced to stay)? ☐ Yes ☒ No

    D. Labor camp (a place where people are forced to work)? ☐ Yes ☒ No

    E. Any other place where people were forced to stay? ☐ Yes ☒ No

17. Were you **EVER** a part of any group, or did you **EVER** help any group, unit, or organization that used a weapon against any person, or threatened to do so? ☐ Yes ☒ No

    A. If you answered "Yes," when you were part of this group, or when you helped this group, did you ever use a weapon against another person? ☐ Yes ☐ No

    B. If you answered "Yes," when you were part of this group, or when you helped this group, did you ever tell another person that you would use a weapon against that person? ☐ Yes ☐ No

18. Did you **EVER** sell, give, or provide weapons to any person, or help another person sell, give, or provide weapons to any person? ☐ Yes ☒ No

    A. If you answered "Yes," did you know that this person was going to use the weapons against another person? ☐ Yes ☐ No

    B. If you answered "Yes," did you know that this person was going to sell or give the weapons to someone who was going to use them against another person? ☐ Yes ☐ No

19. Did you **EVER** receive any type of military, paramilitary (a group of people who act like a military group but are not part of the official military), or weapons training? ☐ Yes ☒ No

20. Did you **EVER** recruit (ask), enlist (sign up), conscript (require), or use any person under 15 years of age to serve in or help an armed force or group? ☐ Yes ☒ No

21. Did you **EVER** use any person under 15 years of age to do anything that helped or supported people in combat? ☐ Yes ☒ No

If any of Item Numbers 22. - 28. apply to you, you must answer "Yes" even if your records have been sealed, expunged, or otherwise cleared. You must disclose this information even if someone, including a judge, law enforcement officer, or attorney, told you that it no longer constitutes a record or told you that you do not have to disclose the information.

22. Have you **EVER** committed, assisted in committing, or attempted to commit, a crime or offense for which you were **NOT** arrested? ☐ Yes ☒ No

23. Have you **EVER** been arrested, cited, or detained by any law enforcement officer (including any immigration official or any official of the U.S. armed forces) for any reason? ☐ Yes ☒ No

24. Have you **EVER** been charged with committing, attempting to commit, or assisting in committing a crime or offense? ☐ Yes ☒ No

25. Have you **EVER** been convicted of a crime or offense? ☐ Yes ☒ No

26. Have you **EVER** been placed in an alternative sentencing or a rehabilitative program (for example, diversion, deferred prosecution, withheld adjudication, deferred adjudication)? ☐ Yes ☒ No

27. A. Have you **EVER** received a suspended sentence, been placed on probation, or been paroled? ☐ Yes ☒ No

   B. If you answered "Yes," have you completed the probation or parole? ☐ Yes ☒ No

28. A. Have you **EVER** been in jail or prison? ☐ Yes ☒ No

   B. If you answered "Yes," how long were you in jail or prison? Years ☐ Months ☐ Days ☐

29. If you answered "No" to **ALL** questions in **Item Numbers 23. - 28.**, then skip this item and go to **Item Number 30.**

   If you answered "Yes" to any question in **Item Numbers 23. - 28.**, then complete this table. If you need extra space, use additional sheets of paper and provide any evidence to support your answers.

Why were you arrested, cited, detained, or charged?	Date arrested, cited, detained, or charged. (mm/dd/yyyy)	Where were you arrested, cited, detained, or charged? (City or Town, State, Country)	Outcome or disposition of the arrest, citation, detention, or charge (no charges filed, charges dismissed, jail, probation, etc.)

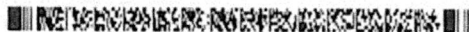

Answer **Item Numbers 30. - 46.** If you answer "Yes" to any of these questions, except **Item Numbers 37.** and **38.**, include a typed or printed explanation on additional sheets of paper and provide any evidence to support your answers.

30. Have you **EVER**:

   A. Been a habitual drunkard? ☐ Yes ☒ No

   B. Been a prostitute, or procured anyone for prostitution? ☐ Yes ☒ No

   C. Sold or smuggled controlled substances, illegal drugs, or narcotics? ☐ Yes ☒ No

   D. Been married to more than one person at the same time? ☐ Yes ☒ No

   E. Married someone in order to obtain an immigration benefit? ☐ Yes ☒ No

   F. Helped anyone to enter, or try to enter, the United States illegally? ☐ Yes ☒ No

   G. Gambled illegally or received income from illegal gambling? ☐ Yes ☒ No

   H. Failed to support your dependents or to pay alimony? ☐ Yes ☒ No

   I. Made any misrepresentation to obtain any public benefit in the United States? ☐ Yes ☒ No

31. Have you **EVER** given any U.S. Government officials **any** information or documentation that was false, fraudulent, or misleading? ☐ Yes ☒ No

32. Have you **EVER** lied to any U.S. Government officials to gain entry or admission into the United States or to gain immigration benefits while in the United States? ☐ Yes ☒ No

33. Have you **EVER** been removed, excluded, or deported from the United States? ☐ Yes ☒ No

34. Have you **EVER** been ordered removed, excluded, or deported from the United States? ☐ Yes ☒ No

35. Have you **EVER** been placed in removal, exclusion, rescission, or deportation proceedings? ☐ Yes ☒ No

36. Are removal, exclusion, rescission, or deportation proceedings (including administratively closed proceedings) **currently** pending against you? ☐ Yes ☒ No

37. Have you **EVER** served in the U.S. armed forces? ☐ Yes ☒ No

38. A. Are you **currently** a member of the U.S. armed forces? ☐ Yes ☒ No

   B. If you answered "Yes," are you scheduled to deploy overseas, including to a vessel, within the next three months? (Refer to the **Address Change** section in the Instructions on how to notify USCIS if you learn of your deployment plans after you file your Form N-400.) ☐ Yes ☐ No

   C. If you answered "Yes," are you **currently** stationed overseas? ☐ Yes ☐ No

39. Have you **EVER** been court-martialed, administratively separated, or disciplined, or have you received an other than honorable discharge, while in the U.S. armed forces? ☐ Yes ☒ No

40. Have you **EVER** been discharged from training or service in the U.S. armed forces because you were an alien? ☐ Yes ☒ No

41. Have you **EVER** left the United States to avoid being drafted in the U.S. armed forces? ☐ Yes ☒ No

42. Have you **EVER** applied for any kind of exemption from military service in the U.S. armed forces? ☐ Yes ☒ No

43. Have you **EVER** deserted from the U.S. armed forces? ☐ Yes ☒ No

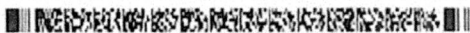

Part 12. Additional Information About You (Person Applying for Naturalization) (continued)

A- 0 6 5 8 0 3 9 2 2

44. **A.** Are you a male who lived in the United States at any time between your 18th and 26th birthdays? ☐ Yes ☒ No
(This does not include living in the United States as a lawful nonimmigrant.)

B. If you answered "Yes," when did you register for the Selective Service? Provide the information below.

Date Registered
(mm/dd/yyyy)

Selective Service
Number

C. If you answered "Yes," but you **did not register** with the Selective Service System and you are:

1. Still under 26 years of age, you must register before you apply for naturalization, and complete the Selective Service information above; **OR**

2. Now 26 to 31 years of age (29 years of age if you are filing under INA section 319(a)), but you did not register with the Selective Service, you must attach a statement explaining why you did not register, and provide a status information letter from the Selective Service.

Answer **Item Numbers 45. - 50.** If you answer "No" to any of these questions, include a typed or printed explanation on additional sheets of paper and provide any evidence to support your answers.

45. Do you support the Constitution and form of Government of the United States? ☐ Yes ☒ No

46. Do you understand the full Oath of Allegiance to the United States? ☐ Yes ☒ No

47. Are you willing to take the full Oath of Allegiance to the United States? ☐ Yes ☒ No

48. If the law requires it, are you willing to bear arms on behalf of the United States? ☐ Yes ☒ No

49. If the law requires it, are you willing to perform noncombatant services in the U.S. armed forces? ☐ Yes ☒ No

50. If the law requires it, are you willing to perform work of national importance under civilian direction? ☐ Yes ☒ No

Part 13. Applicant's Statement, Certification, and Signature

NOTE: Read the **Penalties** section of the Form N-400 Instructions before completing this part.

Applicant's Statement

NOTE: Select the box for either **Item A.** or **B.** in **Item Number 1.** If applicable, select the box for **Item Number 2.**

1. Applicant's Statement Regarding the Interpreter

   A. ☒ I can read and understand English, and I have read and understand every question and instruction on this application and my answer to every question.

   B. ☐ The interpreter named in **Part 14.** read to me every question and instruction on this application and my answer to every question in _____, a language in which I am fluent, and I understood everything.

2. Applicant's Statement Regarding the Preparer

   ☒ At my request, the preparer named in **Part 15.,** 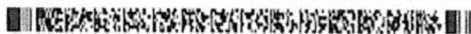 Christopher A. Reed ,
   prepared this application for me based only upon information I provided or authorized.

Applicant's Certification

Copies of any documents I have submitted are exact photocopies of unaltered, original documents, and I understand that USCIS may require that I submit original documents to USCIS at a later date. Furthermore, I authorize the release of any information from any of my records that USCIS may need to determine my eligibility for the immigration benefit that I seek.

I further authorize release of information contained in this application, in supporting documents, and in my USCIS records to other entities and persons where necessary for the administration and enforcement of U.S. immigration laws.

I understand that USCIS will require me to appear for an appointment to take my biometrics (fingerprints, photograph, and/or signature) and, at that time, I will be required to sign an oath reaffirming that:

1) I reviewed and provided or authorized all of the information in my application;

2) I understood all of the information contained in, and submitted with, my application; and

3) All of this information was complete, true, and correct at the time of filing.

I certify, under penalty of perjury, that I provided or authorized all of the information in my application, I understand all of the information contained in, and submitted with, my application, and that all of this information is complete, true, and correct.

Applicant's Signature

3. Applicant's Signature   Date of Signature (mm/dd/yyyy)

➡ | | 09/16/2020

NOTE TO ALL APPLICANTS: If you do not completely fill out this application or fail to submit required documents listed in the Instructions, USCIS may deny your application.

Part 14. Interpreter's Contact Information, Certification, and Signature

Provide the following information about the interpreter.

Interpreter's Full Name

1. Interpreter's Family Name (Last Name)   Interpreter's Given Name (First Name)

2. Interpreter's Business or Organization Name (if any)

Interpreter's Mailing Address

3. Street Number and Name   Apt. Ste. Flr. Number
    ☐   ☐   ☐

    City or Town   State   ZIP Code + 4

    Province   Postal Code   Country

Part 14. Interpreter's Contact Information, Certification, and Signature (continued)

A- [0] [6] [5] [8] [0] [3] [9] [2] [2]

Interpreter's Contact Information

4. Interpreter's Daytime Telephone Number

5. Interpreter's Mobile Telephone Number (if any)

6. Interpreter's Email Address (if any)

Interpreter's Certification

I certify, under penalty of perjury, that:

I am fluent in English and _____, which is the same language specified in **Part 13., Item B.** in **Item Number 1.**, and I have read to this applicant in the identified language every question and instruction on this application and his or her answer to every question. The applicant informed me that he or she understands every instruction, question and answer on the application, including the **Applicant's Certification** and has verified the accuracy of every answer.

Interpreter's Signature

7. Interpreter's Signature

Date of Signature (mm/dd/yyyy)

➡

Part 15. Contact Information, Declaration, and Signature of the Person Preparing This Application, if Other Than the Applicant

Provide the following information about the preparer.

Preparer's Full Name

1. Preparer's Family Name (Last Name)

Reed

Preparer's Given Name (First Name)

Christopher

2. Preparer's Business or Organization Name (if any)

Law Offices of Brian D. Lerner, APC

Preparer's Mailing Address

3. Street Number and Name

3233 E. Broadway

Apt. ☐ Ste. ☐ Flr. ☐ Number

City or Town

Long Beach

State

CA

ZIP Code + 4

90803 -

Province

Postal Code

Country

USA

Part 15. Contact Information, Declaration, and Signature of the Person Preparing This Application, if Other Than the Applicant (continued)

A- | 0 | 6 | 5 | 8 | 0 | 3 | 9 | 2 | 2

Preparer's Contact Information

4. Preparer's Daytime Telephone Number

(562) 495-0554

5. Preparer's Mobile Telephone Number (if any)

N/A

6. Preparer's Email Address (if any)

creed@eimmigration.org

Preparer's Statement

7. A. ☐ I am not an attorney or accredited representative but have prepared this application on behalf of the applicant and with the applicant's consent.

B. ☒ I am an attorney or accredited representative and my representation of the applicant in this case ☒ extends ☐ does not extend beyond the preparation of this application.

NOTE: If you are an attorney or accredited representative whose representation extends beyond preparation of this application, you may be obliged to submit a completed Form G-28, Notice of Entry of Appearance as Attorney or Accredited Representative, with this application.

Preparer's Certification

By my signature, I certify, under penalty of perjury, that I prepared this application at the request of the applicant. The applicant then reviewed this completed application and informed me that he or she understands all of the information contained in, and submitted with, his or her application, including the **Applicant's Certification**, and that all of this information is complete, true, and correct. I completed this application based only on information that the applicant provided to me or authorized me to obtain or use.

Preparer's Signature

8. Preparer's Signature

➡

Date of Signature (mm/dd/yyyy)

09/16/2020

NOTE: Do not complete Parts 16., 17., or 18. until the USCIS Officer instructs you to do so at the interview.

Part 16. Signature at Interview

I swear (affirm) and certify under penalty of perjury under the laws of the United States of America that I know that the contents of this Form N-400, Application for Naturalization, subscribed by me, including corrections number 1 through _____ , are complete, true, and correct. The evidence submitted by me on numbered pages 1 through _____ are complete, true, and correct.

Subscribed to and sworn to (affirmed) before me

USCIS Officer's Printed Name or Stamp

Date of Signature (mm/dd/yyyy)

Applicant's Signature

USCIS Officer's Signature

Part 17. Renunciation of Foreign Titles A- | 0 | 6 | 5 | 8 | 0 | 3 | 9 | 2 | 2 |

If you answered "Yes" to **Part 12.**, **Items A.** and **B.** in **Item Number 4.**, then you must affirm the following before a USCIS officer:

I further renounce the title of _____ which I have heretofore held; or
(list titles)

I further renounce the order of nobility of _____ to which I have heretofore belonged.
(list order of nobility)

Applicant's Printed Name

Applicant's Signature

USCIS Officer's Printed Name

USCIS Officer's Signature

Date of Signature (mm/dd/yyyy)

Part 18. Oath of Allegiance

If your application is approved, you will be scheduled for a public oath ceremony at which time you will be required to take the following Oath of Allegiance immediately prior to becoming a naturalized citizen. By signing below you acknowledge your willingness and ability to take this oath:

I hereby declare on oath, that I absolutely and entirely renounce and abjure all allegiance and fidelity to any foreign prince, potentate, state, or sovereignty, of whom or which I have heretofore been a subject or citizen;

that I will support and defend the Constitution and laws of the United States of America against all enemies, foreign, and domestic;

that I will bear true faith and allegiance to the same;

that I will bear arms on behalf of the United States when required by the law;

that I will perform noncombatant service in the armed forces of the United States when required by the law;

that I will perform work of national importance under civilian direction when required by the law; and

that I take this obligation freely, without any mental reservation or purpose of evasion; so help me God.

Applicant's Printed Name

Family Name (Last Name)	Given Name (First Name)	Middle Name (if applicable)

Applicant's Signature

Date of Signature (mm/dd/yyyy)

Addendum

ABDULHUSAIN, Hussein Mukhtar Taher, Form: N-400, A# 065803922 , 09/16/2020 (Page 1)

Part 8: Additional Employment & Education History:

Employer: Galini; Address: 2228 Glendale Galleria, City: Glendale, State/Province: CA, Zip Code/Postal Code: 91210, Country: USA; From: 09/01/2018, To: 03/15/2019
Occupation: Business Development Consultant

EXHIBITS

EXHIBIT '1':
Applicant's Permanent Resident Card

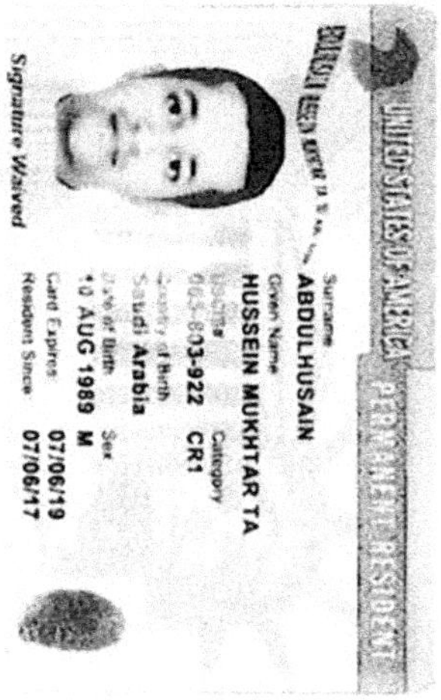
UNITED STATES OF AMERICA
PERMANENT RESIDENT
Surname
ABDULHUSAIN
Given Name
HUSSEIN MUKHTAR TA
Category
CR1
Saudi Arabia
Date of Birth
Sex
10 AUG 1989
M
Card Expires
07/06/19
Resident Since
07/06/17
Signature Waived

P<USA...
C1USA06580392231OE02520325565<<
8908102M1907069SAU<<<<<<<<<<<<4
ABDULHUSAIN<<HUSSEIN<MUKHTAR<T

EXHIBIT '2':
Applicant's Passport

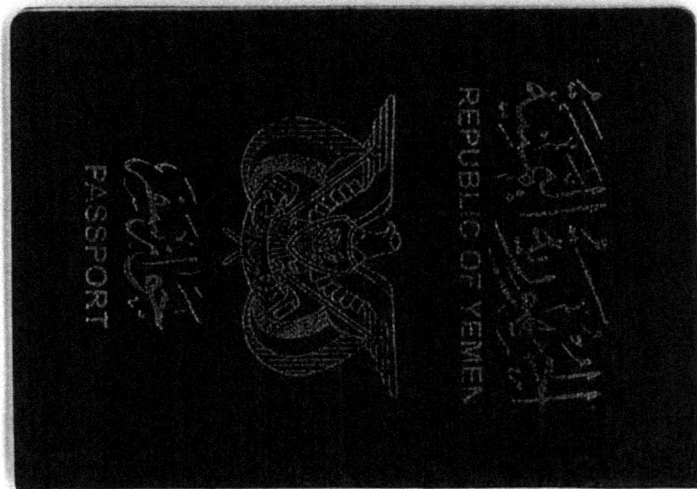

06157582

REPUBLIC OF YEMEN
MINISTRY OF INTERIOR
IMMIGRATION, PASSPORTS AND NATURALIZATION AUTHORITY

On behalf of the Minister of Foreign Affairs interested authorities are requested to allow the bearer to pass freely and without hindrance and to grant him any assistance and protection which he may need.

Passport Director
or General Director

REPUBLIC OF YEMEN
PASSPORT جواز سفر

الجمهورية اليمنية

TYPE P	COUNTRY CODE YEM	PASSPORT No 06157582
SURNAME ABDULHUSAIN		حسين مختار طاهر
GIVEN NAMES HUSSEIN MUKHTAR TAHER		عبدالحسين
PROFESSION FINANCIAL ANALYST		محلل مالي
PLACE OF BIRTH JEDDAH – KSA		السعودية - جده
DATE OF BIRTH 10/08/1989	SEX M	1989/08/10
DATE OF ISSUE 11/03/2015	DATE OF EXPIRY 11/03/2021	2021/03/11 2015/03/11
ISSUING AUTHORITY JEDDAH		جده

P<YEMABDULHUSAIN<<HUSSEIN<MUKHTAR<TAHER<<<<<
06157582<2YEM8908102M2103112<<<<<<<<<<<<04

37 | P a g e

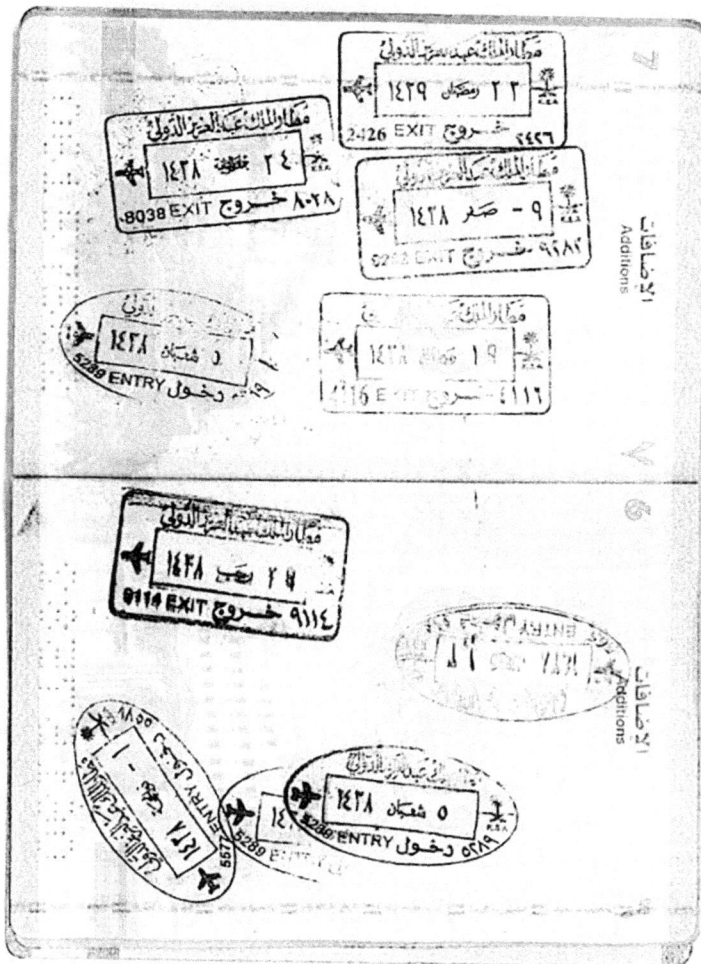

VISA UNITED STATES OF AMERICA

Issuing Post Name	Control Number
JEDDAH	20151404640001
Surname	
ABDULHUSAIN	
Given Name	Visa Type /Class
HUSSEIN MUKHTAR TAHER	R B1/B2
Passport Number Sex	Birth Date Nationality
06157582 M	10AUG1989 YEM
Entries Issue Date	Expiration Date
M 21MAY2015	19MAY2016 1010
Annotation	
	K2042119

VNUSAABDULHUSAIN<<HUSSEIN<MUKHTAR<TAHER<<<<<
06157582<2YEM8908102M1605192B3JDD048C5840109

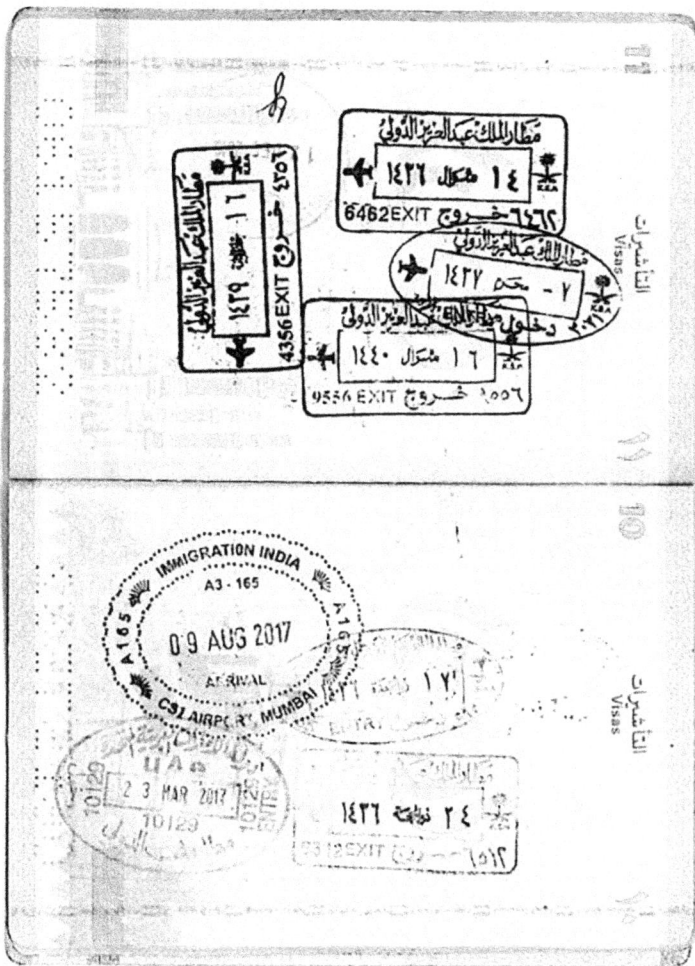

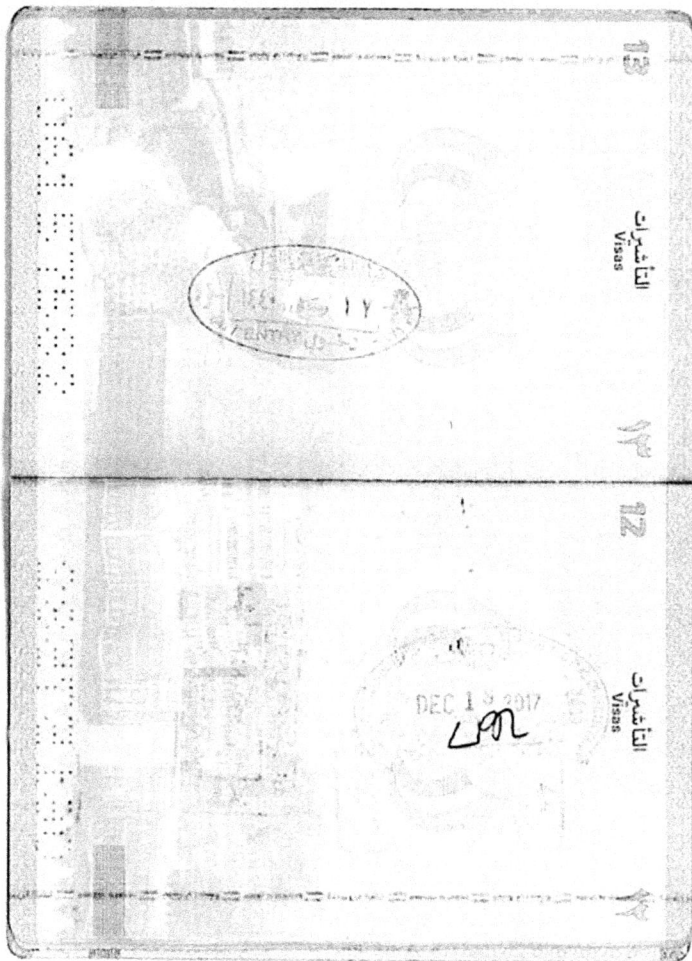

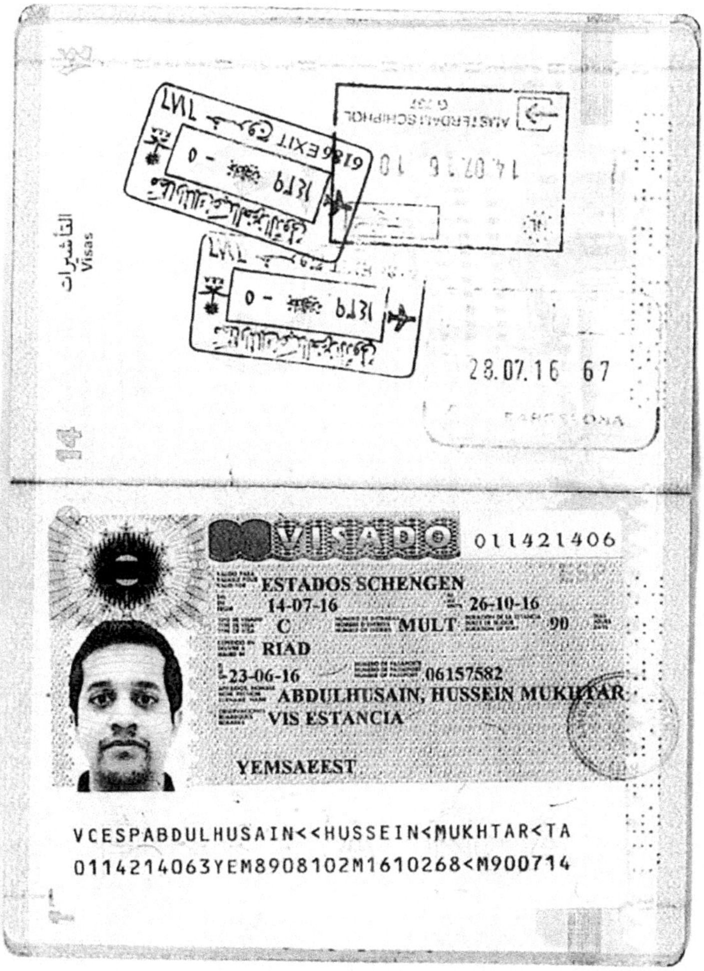
التأشيرات
Visas
14
28.07.16 67
VISADO 011421406
ESTADOS SCHENGEN
14-07-16
26-10-16
C
MULT
90
RIAD
23-06-16
06157582
ABDULHUSAIN, HUSSEIN MUKHTAR
VIS ESTANCIA
YEMSAEEST
VCESPABDULHUSAIN<<HUSSEIN<MUKHTAR<TA
0114214063YEM8908102M1610268<M900714

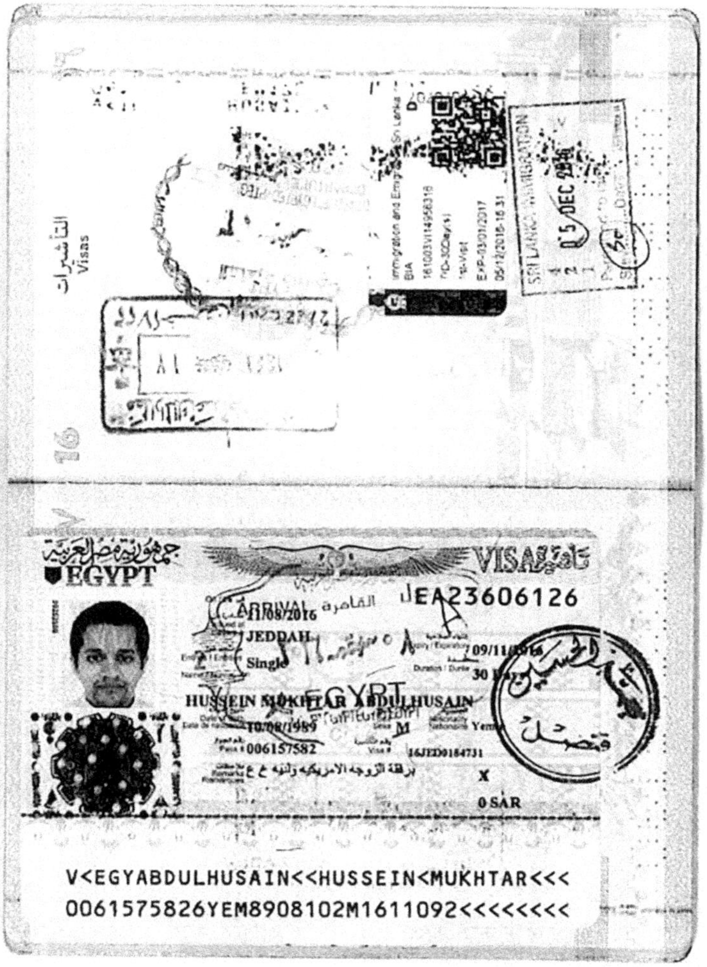

الشيرات
Visas

VISA تأشيرة

EGYPT

ARRIVAL 08/2016
JEDDAH
Single

EA23606126

القاهرة

09/11/2016
30

HUSSEIN MUKHTAR ABDULHUSAIN
10/08/1989
006157582

GYPT
M
16JED0184731

Yem

X

0 SAR

V<EGYABDULHUSAIN<<HUSSEIN<MUKHTAR<<<
0061575826YEM8908102M1611092<<<<<<<<

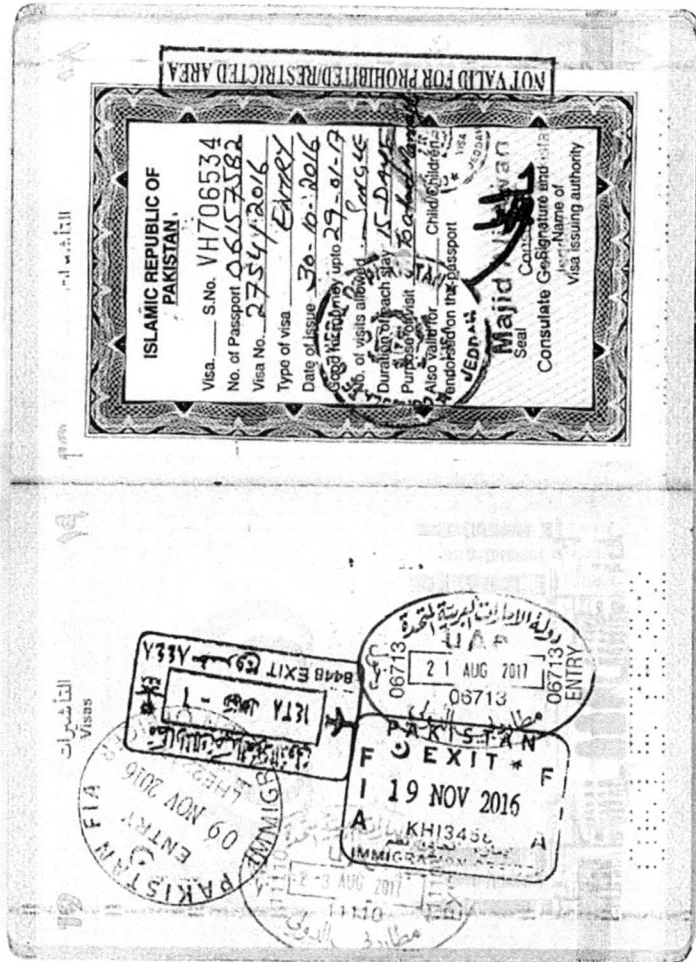

KINGDOM OF THAILAND

TYPE OF VISA	CATEGORY	PORT OF ENTRY	FEE
Tourist	TR S		0 SAR

ISSUED AT: JEDDAH
DATE OF ISSUE: 21 Dec 2016

ENTER BEFORE: 20 Mar 2017
PASSPORT NO: 06157582
NO. OF ACCOMPANYING CHILDREN: 0

REMARKS: Employment Prohibited

C 2700394

V<THAABDULHUSAIN<<HUSSEIN<MUKHTAR<TA
06157582<2YEM8908102M17032052700394<

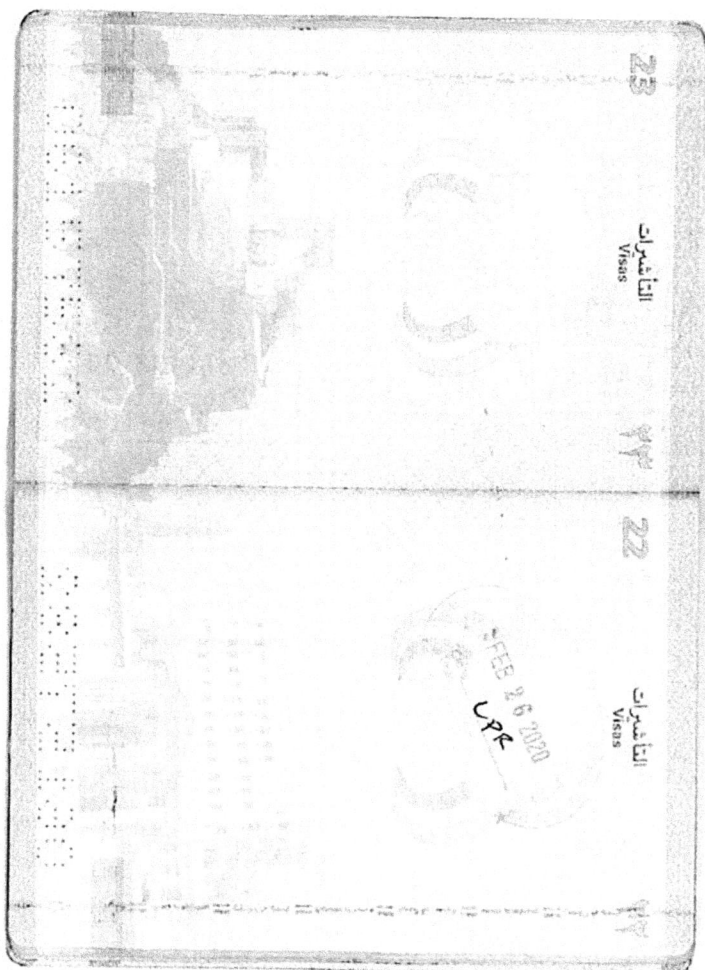

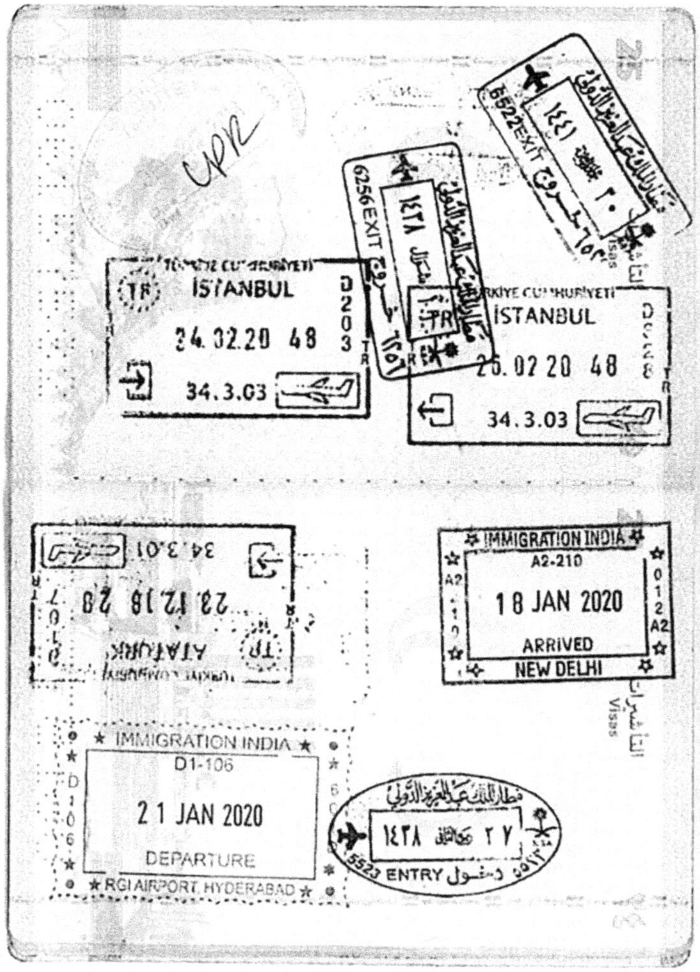

CYPR

TÜRKİYE CUMHURİYETİ
TR İSTANBUL D203
24.02.20 48
34.3.03

6256 EXIT ١٤٣١

TÜRKİYE CUMHURİYETİ
TR İSTANBUL D2028
25.02.20 48
34.3.03

6522 EXIT ١٤٣١
١٠

34.3.01
23.12.18 28
TR ATATÜRK

★ IMMIGRATION INDIA ★
A2-210
18 JAN 2020
ARRIVED
NEW DELHI

★ IMMIGRATION INDIA ★
D1-106
21 JAN 2020
DEPARTURE
★ RGI AIRPORT, HYDERABAD ★

مطار الملك عبد العزيز الدولي
٢٧ ١٤٣١
ENTRY دخول

TÜRKIYE
CUMHURİYETİ   VİZE   51 971234

VİZE TÜRÜ
TYPE OF VISA   Turistik / Tourism

GEÇERLİK SÜRESİ
PERIOD OF VALIDITY   05.04.2017   FROM   04.07.2017   TUR
KALAN ÜNTL.

REPUBLIC OF TURKEY   GİRİŞ SAYISI
NUMBER OF ENTRIES   Tek Giriş / Single Entry   HAMIT SÜRESİ
DURATION OF STAY

VEREN MAKAM
ISSUING AUTHORITY   T.C. Cidde BK

TANZIM TARİHİ
ISSUED ON   05.04.2017   PASAPORT
PASSPORT   06157582

ADI - SOYADI
NAME - SURNAME   HUSSEIN MUKHTAR TAHER ABDULHUSAIN

AÇIKLAMALAR
REMARKS

V<TURABDULHUSAIN<<HUSSEIN<MUKHTAR<TA
06157582<2YEM1704051M2103112<<<<<<<0

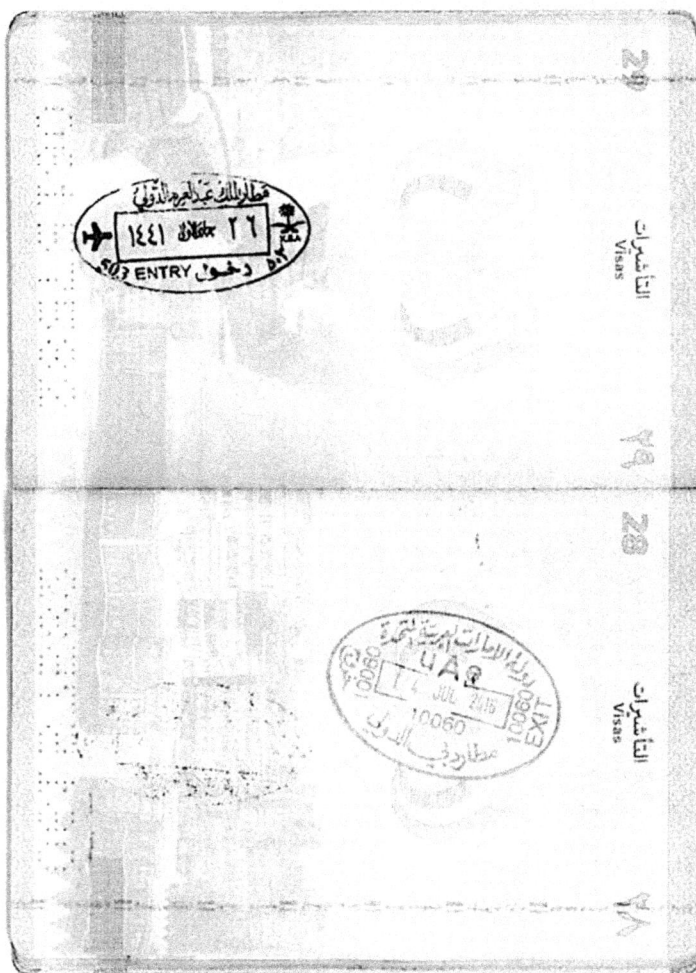

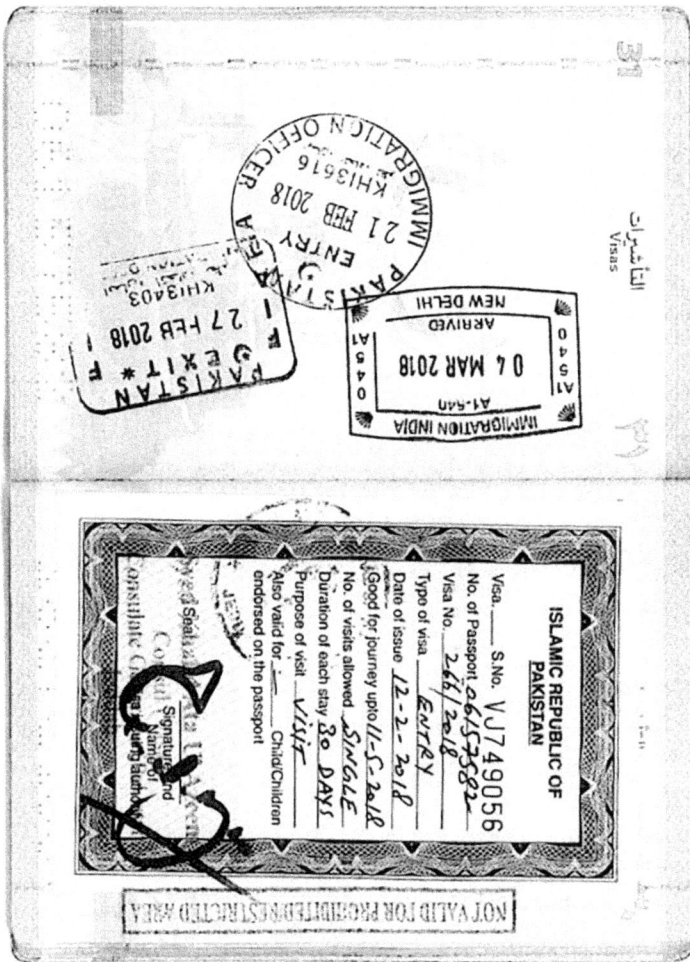

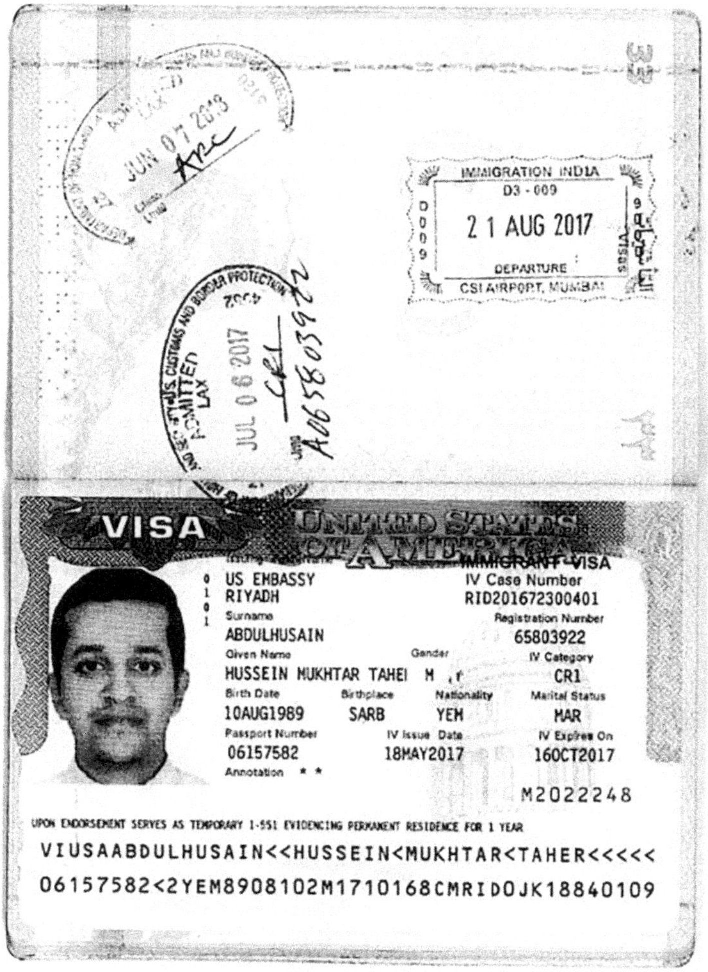

IMMIGRATION INDIA
D3 - 009
21 AUG 2017
DEPARTURE
CSI AIRPORT, MUMBAI

U.S. CUSTOMS AND BORDER PROTECTION
ADMITTED
LAX
JUL 06 2017
CR1
A065803922

JUN 07 2018

VISA UNITED STATES OF AMERICA
IMMIGRANT VISA

US EMBASSY
RIYADH
IV Case Number
RID201672300401
Surname
ABDULHUSAIN
Registration Number
65803922
Given Name
HUSSEIN MUKHTAR TAHEI
Gender
M
IV Category
CR1
Birth Date
10AUG1989
Birthplace
SARB
Nationality
YEM
Marital Status
MAR
Passport Number
06157582
IV Issue Date
18MAY2017
IV Expires On
16OCT2017
Annotation * *
M2022248

UPON ENDORSEMENT SERVES AS TEMPORARY I-551 EVIDENCING PERMANENT RESIDENCE FOR 1 YEAR

VIUSAABDULHUSAIN<<HUSSEIN<MUKHTAR<TAHER<<<<<

06157582<2YEM8908102M1710168CMRIDOJK18840109

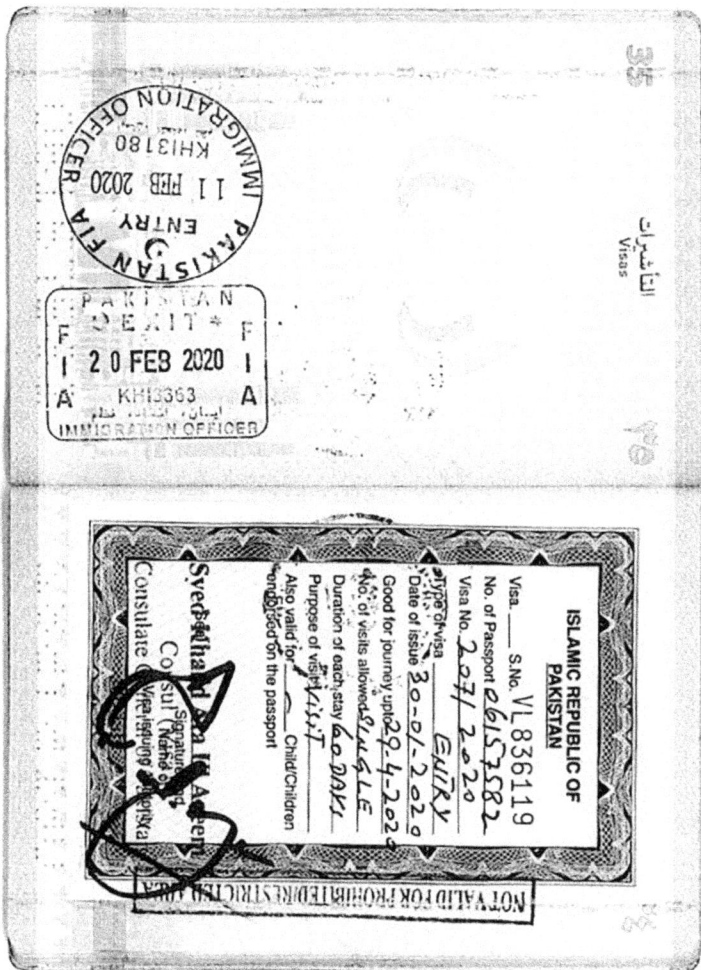

ISLAMIC REPUBLIC OF
PAKISTAN

Visa _____ S.No. VL836119
No. of Passport 0615フ5582
Visa No. 2.07/2020
Type of visa _____ ENTRY
Date of issue 2.07/2020
Good for journey upto 29-4-2020
No. of visits allowed SINGLE
Duration of each stay 60 DAYS
Purpose of visit VISIT
Also valid for _____
_____ Child/Children
endorsed on the passport

Syed Shahid Ali Anjem
Consul (Name)
Consulate of Pakistan

NOT VALID FOR PROHIBITED/RESTRICTED AREA

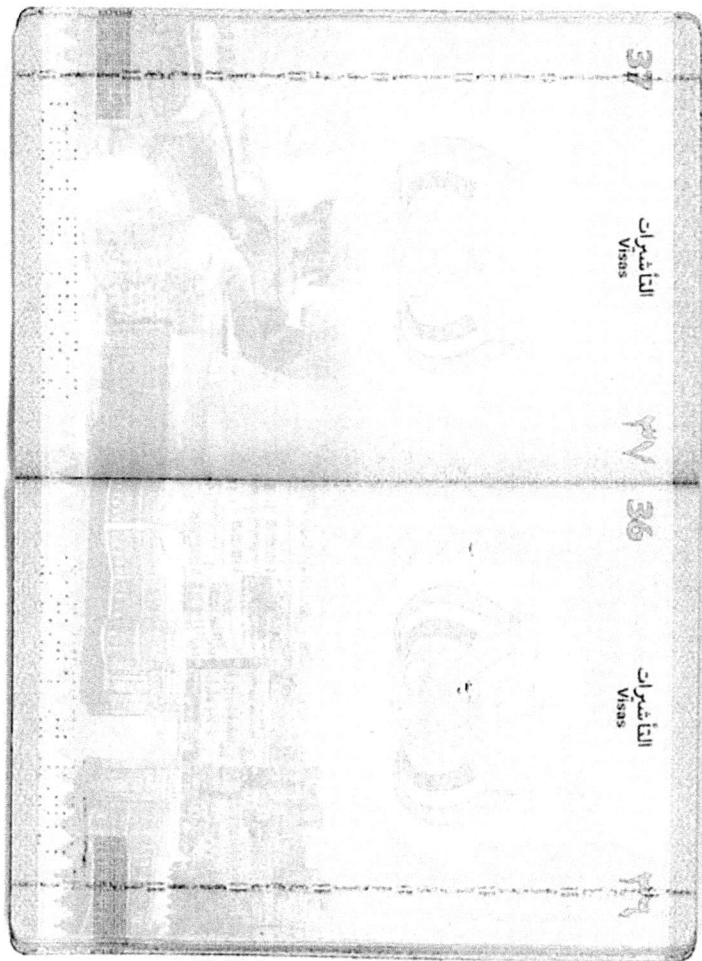

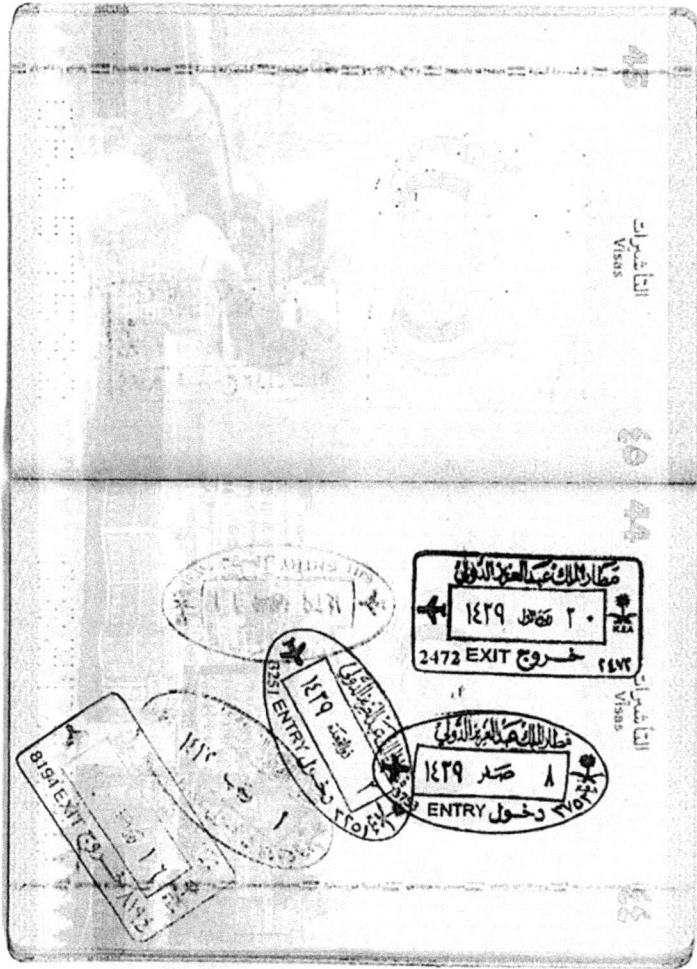

TÜRKIYE
CUMHURIYETI   V I Z E   51 995428

VİZE TÜRÜ TYPE OF VISA	Turistik / Tourism		
GEÇERLİLİK SÜRESİ PERIOD OF VALIDITY	11.10.2017	FROM	09.01.2018
GİRİŞ SAYISI NUMBER OF ENTRIES	Tek Giriş / Single Entry	TRANSİT SÜRESİ DURATION OF STAY	10
VEREN MAKAM ISSUING AUTHORITY	T.C. Cidde BK		
TANZİM TARİHİ ISSUED ON	11.10.2017	PASAPORT NO PASSPORT NO	06157582
ADI - SOYADI NAME - SURNAME	HUSSEIN MUKHTAR TAHER ABDULHUSAIN		
AÇIKLAMALAR REMARKS			

REPUBLIC OF TURKEY

V<TURABDULHUSAIN<<HUSSEIN<MUKHTAR<TA
06157582<2YEM1710113M2103112<<<<<<<4

Instructions

1. Passports of the Republic of Yemen are t[...] Immigration, Passports and Naturalization Au[...] offices or by the Diplomatic Missions and Con[...] Republic accredited abroad.

2. This passport contains 48 pages.

Caution

This passport is an important document. It sho[...] ved securely so that it does not fall into the pos[...] unauthorized person. Its loss or destructio[...] reported immediately to the issuing author[...] nearest Diplomatic Missions for the Republic[...] any authorized representative. Replacement d[...] be issued only after thorough investigation.

EXHIBIT '3':
Applicant's Marriage Certificate

EXHIBIT '4':
Applicant's Spouse's Naturalization Certificate

THE UNITED STATES OF AMERICA

CERTIFICATE OF NATURALIZATION

No. 37 292524

Personal description of holder as of date of naturalization:

Date of birth: OCTOBER 24, 1987

Sex: FEMALE

Height: 5 *feet* 2 *inches*

Marital status: SINGLE

Country of former nationality: PAKISTAN

USCIS Registration No. A055541250

I certify that the description given is true, and that the photograph affixed hereto is a likeness of me.

(Complete and true signature of holder)

Be it known that, pursuant to an application filed with the Secretary of Homeland Security

at: SANTA ANA, CALIFORNIA

The Secretary having found that: SHARISH BELAL KHANDIA

residing at: GARDEN GROVE, CALIFORNIA

having complied in all respects with all of the applicable provisions of the naturalization laws of the United States, being entitled to be admitted as a citizen of the United States, and having taken the oath of allegiance at a ceremony conducted by US DISTRICT COURT CENTRAL DISTRICT

at: LOS ANGELES, CALIFORNIA *on:* MARCH 18, 2015

such person is admitted as a citizen of the United States of America.

U.S. Citizenship and Immigration Services

ALTERATION OR MISUSE OF THIS DOCUMENT IS A FEDERAL OFFENSE AND PUNISHABLE BY LAW

DEPARTMENT OF HOMELAND SECURITY

FORM N-550 (Rev. 06/12)

EXHIBIT '5':
Applicant's Sons' Birth Certificate

COUNTY OF ORANGE
HEALTH CARE AGENCY

1052019550581

CERTIFICATE OF LIVE BIRTH
STATE OF CALIFORNIA
USE BLACK INK ONLY

1201930503175

THIS CHILD	1A. NAME OF CHILD - FIRST: AYAAN	1B. MIDDLE: HUSSEIN		1C. LAST: ABDULHUSAIN	
	2. SEX: MALE	3A. THIS BIRTH SINGLE, TWIN ETC: SINGLE	3B. IF MULTIPLE, THIS CHILD 1ST, 2ND, ETC: -	4A. DATE OF BIRTH: 04/05/2019	4B. HOUR - 24 HOUR CLOCK TIME: 0312

PLACE OF BIRTH	5A. PLACE OF BIRTH - NAME OF HOSPITAL OR FACILITY: ORANGE COAST MEMORIAL MED CTR	5B. STREET ADDRESS - STREET AND NUMBER, OR LOCATION: 9920 TALBERT AVENUE
	5C. CITY: FOUNTAIN VALLEY	5D. COUNTY: ORANGE

NAME OF PARENT	6A. NAME OF PARENT - FIRST: HUSSEIN	6B. MIDDLE: MUKHTAR TAHER	6C. LAST - BIRTH NAME: ABDULHUSAIN	☑ FATHER	7. BIRTHPLACE - STATE/COUNTRY: SAUDI ARABIA	8. DATE OF BIRTH: 08/10/1989
NAME OF PARENT	9A. NAME OF PARENT - FIRST: SHARISH	9B. MIDDLE: BELAL	9C. LAST - BIRTH NAME: KHANDIA	☑ MOTHER	10. BIRTHPLACE - STATE/COUNTRY: PAKISTAN	11. DATE OF BIRTH: 10/24/1987

INFORMANT AND BIRTH CERTIFICATION	I CERTIFY THAT I HAVE REVIEWED THE STATED INFORMATION AND THAT IT IS TRUE AND CORRECT TO THE BEST OF MY KNOWLEDGE 12A. PARENT OR OTHER INFORMANT - SIGNATURE: HUSSEIN MUKHTAR TAHER ABDULHUSAIN SHARISH KHANDIA ABDULHUSAIN	FATHER MOTHER	12B. DATE SIGNED: 04/08/2019 04/08/2019
	I CERTIFY THAT THE CHILD WAS BORN ALIVE AT THE DATE, HOUR, AND PLACE STATED 13A. ATTENDANT/CERTIFIER - SIGNATURE AND DEGREE OR TITLE: LEANNE NGUYEN, BIRTH CLERK	13B. LICENSE NUMBER: A90651	13C. DATE SIGNED: 04/08/2019
	13D. TYPED NAME, TITLE AND MAILING ADDRESS OF ATTENDANT: CAROLINE ALANA CONNER, MD 9940 TALBERT AVE 303, FOUNTAIN VALLEY, CA 92708	14. TYPED NAME AND TITLE OF CERTIFIER IF OTHER THAN ATTENDANT: LEANNE NGUYEN, BIRTH CLERK	

LOCAL REGISTRAR	15A. DATE OF DEATH:	15B. STATE FILE NO - STATE USE ONLY:	16. LOCAL REGISTRAR - SIGNATURE: NICHOLE QUICK M.D.	17. DATE ACCEPTED FOR REGISTRATION: 04/08/2019

EXHIBIT '6':
Applicant's Joint 2018-2019 Income Tax Returns and W-2s

Form W-2 Wage and Tax Statement — 2018

Copy B – To Be Filed With Employee's FEDERAL Tax Return.
This information is being furnished to the Internal Revenue Service.

OMB No. 1545-0008

Department of the Treasury – Internal Revenue Service

c Employer's name, address, and ZIP code

GALLINI OF CENTURY CITY INC
8500 BEVERLY BLVD
SUITE 647
LOS ANGELES, CA 90048

e Employee's name, address, and ZIP code

HUSSEIN MUKHTAR T ABDULHUSAIN
14152 Flower St
Apt K4
GARDEN GROVE, CA 92843

Box	Description	Amount
1	Wages, tips, other compensation	11000.00
2	Federal income tax withheld	380.38
3	Social security wages	11000.00
4	Social security tax withheld	682.00
5	Medicare wages and tips	11000.00
6	Medicare tax withheld	159.50
14	Other	CASDI 110.00

b Employer identification number (EIN): 27-4520008
a Employee's social security number: 617-75-5679

15 State CA Employer's state ID number 003-9249-8 16 State wages, tips, etc. 11000.00 17 State income tax 103.07

Form W-2 Wage and Tax Statement — 2018

Copy C – For EMPLOYEE'S RECORDS (See Notice to Employee on the back of Copy B.)

OMB No. 1545-0008

Department of the Treasury – Internal Revenue Service

c Employer's name, address, and ZIP code

GALLINI OF CENTURY CITY INC
8500 BEVERLY BLVD
SUITE 647
LOS ANGELES, CA 90048

e Employee's name, address, and ZIP code

HUSSEIN MUKHTAR T ABDULHUSAIN
14152 Flower St
Apt K4
GARDEN GROVE, CA 92843

Box	Description	Amount
1	Wages, tips, other compensation	11000.00
2	Federal income tax withheld	380.38
3	Social security wages	11000.00
4	Social security tax withheld	682.00
5	Medicare wages and tips	11000.00
6	Medicare tax withheld	159.50
14	Other	CASDI 110.00

b Employer identification number (EIN): 27-4520008
a Employee's social security number: 617-75-5679

This information is being furnished to the Internal Revenue Service. If you are required to file a tax return, a negligence penalty or other sanction may be imposed on you if this income is taxable and you fail to report it.

15 State CA Employer's state ID number 003-9249-8 16 State wages, tips, etc. 11000.00 17 State income tax 103.07

Form W-2 Wage and Tax Statement — 2018

Copy 2 – To Be Filed With Employee's State, City, or Local Income Tax Return.

OMB No. 1545-0008

Department of the Treasury – Internal Revenue Service

c Employer's name, address, and ZIP code

GALLINI OF CENTURY CITY INC
8500 BEVERLY BLVD
SUITE 647
LOS ANGELES, CA 90048

e Employee's name, address, and ZIP code

HUSSEIN MUKHTAR T ABDULHUSAIN
14152 Flower St
Apt K4
GARDEN GROVE, CA 92843

Box	Description	Amount
1	Wages, tips, other compensation	11000.00
2	Federal income tax withheld	380.38
3	Social security wages	11000.00
4	Social security tax withheld	682.00
5	Medicare wages and tips	11000.00
6	Medicare tax withheld	159.50
14	Other	CASDI 110.00

b Employer identification number (EIN): 27-4520008
a Employee's social security number: 617-75-5679

15 State CA Employer's state ID number 003-9249-8 16 State wages, tips, etc. 11000.00 17 State income tax 103.07

Form W-2 Wage and Tax Statement — 2018

Copy 2 – To Be Filed With Employee's State, City, or Local Income Tax Return.

OMB No. 1545-0008

Department of the Treasury – Internal Revenue Service

c Employer's name, address, and ZIP code

GALLINI OF CENTURY CITY INC
8500 BEVERLY BLVD
SUITE 647
LOS ANGELES, CA 90048

e Employee's name, address, and ZIP code

HUSSEIN MUKHTAR T ABDULHUSAIN
14152 Flower St
Apt K4
GARDEN GROVE, CA 92843

Box	Description	Amount
1	Wages, tips, other compensation	11000.00
2	Federal income tax withheld	380.38
3	Social security wages	11000.00
4	Social security tax withheld	682.00
5	Medicare wages and tips	11000.00
6	Medicare tax withheld	159.50
14	Other	CASDI 110.00

b Employer identification number (EIN): 27-4520008
a Employee's social security number: 617-75-5679

15 State CA Employer's state ID number 003-9249-8 16 State wages, tips, etc. 11000.00 17 State income tax 103.07

Form 1040
Department of the Treasury - Internal Revenue Service (99)
U.S. Individual Income Tax Return | **2018** | OMB No. 1545-0074 | IRS Use Only - Do not write or staple in this space.

Filing status: ☐ Single ☒ Married filing jointly ☐ Married filing separately ☐ Head of household ☐ Qualifying widow(er)

Your first name and initial	Last name	Your social security number
HUSSEIN MUKHTAR T	ABDULHUSAIN	617-75-5679

Your standard deduction: ☐ Someone can claim you as a dependent ☐ You were born before January 2, 1954 ☐ You are blind

If a joint return, spouse's first name and initial	Last name	Spouse's social security number
SHARISH KHANDIA	ABDULHUSAIN	730-18-6921

Spouse standard deduction: ☐ Someone can claim your spouse as a dependent ☐ Spouse was born before January 2, 1954 | ☒ Full-year health care coverage

☐ Spouse is blind ☐ Spouse itemizes on a separate return or you were dual-status alien | or exempt (see inst.)

Home address (number and street). If you have a P.O. box, see instructions. | Apt. no. | Presidential Election Campaign (see inst)

2447 W ORANGE AVE | ☐ You ☐ Spouse

City, town or post office, state, and ZIP code. If you have a foreign address, attach Schedule 6. | If more than four dependents,

ANAHEIM, CA 92804 | see inst. and ✓ here ▶ ☐

Dependents (see instructions)

(1) First name Last name	(2) Social security number	(3) Relationship to you	(4) ✓ if qualifies for (see inst):
			Child tax credit Credit for other dependents
			☐ ☐
			☐ ☐
			☐ ☐
			☐ ☐

Sign Here

Under penalties of perjury, I declare that I have examined this return and accompanying schedules and statements, and to the best of my knowledge and belief, they are true, correct, and complete. Declaration of preparer (other than taxpayer) is based on all information of which preparer has any knowledge.

Joint return? See instructions. Keep a copy for your records.

Your signature	Date	Your occupation	If the IRS sent you an Identity Protection Pin, enter it here (see inst)
		FINANCIAL ANALYSTS	
Spouse's signature. If a joint return, **both** must sign.	Date	Spouse's occupation	If the IRS sent you an Identity Protection Pin, enter it here (see inst)
		HOUSE WIFE	

Paid Preparer Use Only

Preparer's name	Preparer's signature	PTIN	Firm's EIN	Check if:
Thu Le		P02145227	22-3677427	☐ 3rd Party Designee
Firm's name ▶ Jackson Hewitt Tax Service		Phone no. (657) 235-3889		☐ Self-employed
Firm's address ▶ 11822 Gilbert St		Garden Grove	CA	92841

For Disclosure, Privacy Act, and Paperwork Reduction Act Notice, see separate instructions. | Form **1040** (2018)

Form 1040 (2018) | Page 2

1	Wages, salaries, tips, etc. Attach Form(s) W-2.		**1**	11,000
2a	Tax-exempt interest	**2a**	b Taxable interest	**2b**
3a	Qualified dividends.	**3a**	b Ordinary dividends	**3b**
4a	IRAs, pensions and annuities . . .	**4a**	b Taxable amount	**4b**
5a	Social security benefits.	**5a**	b Taxable amount	**5b**
6	Total income. Add lines 1 through 5. Add any amount from Schedule 1, line 22.		**6**	11,000
7	Adjusted gross income. If you have no adjustments to income, enter the amount from line 6; otherwise, subtract Schedule 1, line 36 from line 6.		**7**	11,000

Standard Deduction for -
● Single or Married filing separately $12,000
● Married filing jointly or Qualifying widow(er), $24,000
● Head of household $18,000
● If you checked any box under Standard deduction, see instructions.

8	Standard deduction or Itemized deductions (from Schedule A)		**8**	24,000
9	Qualified business income deduction (see instructions)		**9**	
10	Taxable income. Subtract lines 8 and 9 from line 7. If zero or less, enter -0-. . .		**10**	NONE
11	a Tax (see inst) ___NONE___ (Check if any from: a ☐ Form(s) 8814 b ☐ Form 4972 c ☐)			
	b Add any amount from Schedule 2 and check here . . . . ▶ ☒		**11**	600
12	a Child tax credit/credit for other dependents ___ b Add any amount from Schedule 3 and check here ▶ ☐		**12**	
13	Subtract line 12 from line 11. If zero or less, enter 0.		**13**	600
14	Other taxes. Attach Schedule 4.		**14**	
15	Total tax. Add lines 13 through 14.		**15**	600
16	Federal income tax withheld from Forms W-2 and 1099.		**16**	380
17	Refundable credits: a EIC (see ins) ___519___ b Sch 8812 ___ c Form 8863 ___			
	Add any amount from Schedule 5 ___NONE___		**17**	519
18	Add lines 16 and 17. These are your total payments.		**18**	899

Refund

19	If line 18 is more than line 15, subtract line 15 from line 18. This is the amount you overpaid		**19**	299
20 a	Amount of line 19 you want refunded to you. If Form 8888 is attached, check here . . ▶ ☐		**20a**	299

Direct deposit? See instructions ▶ b Routing number ******358 ▶ c Type: ☒ Checking ☐ Savings

▶ d Account number *******8506

21	Amount of line 19 you want applied to your 2019 estimated tax ▶	**21**	

Amount You Owe

22	Amount you owe. Subtract line 18 from line 15. For details on how to pay, see instructions . . . . ▶	**22**	
23	Estimated tax penalty (see instructions)	**23**	NONE

Go to www.irs.gov/Form1040 for instructions and latest information. | NYA | Form **1040** (2018)

SCHEDULE 2 (Form 1040) Department of the Treasury Internal Revenue Service	Tax ▶ Attach to Form 1040. ▶ Go to *www.irs.gov/Form1040* for instructions and the latest information.	OMB No. 1545-0074 2018 Attachment Sequence No. 02

Name(s) shown on Form 1040	Your social security number
HUSSEIN MUKHTAR T & SHARISH KHANDIA ABDULHUSAIN	617-75-5679

Tax	38–44	Reserved	38–44	
	45	Alternative minimum tax. Attach Form 6251	45	
	46	Excess advance premium tax credit repayment. Attach Form 8962	46	600
	47	Add the amounts in the far right column. Enter here and include on Form 1040, line 11	47	600

For Paperwork Reduction Act Notice, see your tax return instructions.　F 12/13/18　Cat. No. 71478U　MXA　Schedule 2 (Form 1040) 2018

SCHEDULE 6
(Form 1040)

Department of the Treasury
Internal Revenue Service

Foreign Address and Third Party Designee

▶ Attach to Form 1040.
▶ Go to *www.irs.gov/Form1040* for instructions and the latest information.

OMB No. 1545-0074

2018

Attachment
Sequence No. **05A**

Name(s) shown on Form 1040	Your social security number
HUSSEIN MUKHTAR T & SHARISH KHANDIA ABDULHUSAIN	617-75-5679

Foreign Address	Foreign country name	Foreign province/county	Foreign postal code

Third Party Designee	Do you want to allow another person to discuss this return with the IRS (see instructions)? [X] **Yes.** Complete below. [ ] **No**		
	Designee's name ▶ Tonya Bixler	Phone no. ▶ (562) 506-1009	Personal identification number (PIN) ▶ 94597

For Paperwork Reduction Act Notice, see your tax return instructions. MXA Cat. No. 71483N F 12/13/18 Schedule 6 (Form 1040) 2018

Paid Preparer's Due Diligence Checklist

Earned Income Credit (EIC), American Opportunity Tax Credit (AOTC), Child Tax Credit (CTC) (including the Additional Child Tax Credit (ACTC) and Credit for Other Dependents (ODC)), and Head of Household (HOH) Filing Status.

▶ To be completed by preparer and filed with Form 1040,1040NR, 1040SS or 1040PR.
▶ Go to www.irs.gov/form8867 for instructions and the latest information.

OMB No. 1545-1629

2018

Attachment
Sequence No. 70

Taxpayer name(s) shown on return	Taxpayer identification number
HUSSEIN MUKHTAR T & SHARISH KHANDIA ABDULHUSAIN	617-75-5679

Enter preparer's name and PTIN

Thu Le	p02145227

Part I — Due Diligence Requirements

	Please check the appropriate box for the credit(s) and/or HOH filing status claimed on this return and complete the related Parts I - V for the benefit(s), and/or HOH filing status claimed (check all that apply).	EIC	CTC/ ACTC/ODC	AOTC	HOH
		☒	☐	☐	☐

			Yes	No	N/A
1	Did you complete the return based on information for tax year 2018 provided by the taxpayer or reasonably obtained by you?		☒ Yes	☐ No	
2	If credits are claimed on the return, did you complete the applicable EIC and/ or CTC/ACTC/ODC worksheets found in the Form 1040, 1040SS, 1040PR, or 1040NR instructions, and/or the AOTC worksheet found in the Form 8863 instructions, or your own worksheet(s) that provides the same information, and all related forms and schedules for each credit claimed?		☒ Yes	☐ No	☐ N/A
3	Did you satisfy the knowledge requirement? To meet the knowledge requirement, you must do both of the following: ● Interview the taxpayer, ask questions, and document the taxpayer's responses to determine that the taxpayer is eligible to claim the credit(s) and/or HOH filing status. ● Review information to determine that the taxpayer is eligible to claim the credit(s) and/or HOH filing status and the amount of any credit(s) claimed.		☒ Yes	☐ No	
4	Did any information provided by the taxpayer or a third party for use in preparing the return, or information reasonably known to you, appear to be incorrect, incomplete, or inconsistent? (If "yes," answer questions 4a and 4b. If "no," go to question 5.)		☐ Yes	☒ No	
a	Did you make reasonable inquiries to determine the correct, complete and consistent information?		☐ Yes	☐ No	
b	Did you document your inquiries? (Documentation should include the questions you asked, whom you asked, when you asked, the information that was provided, and the impact the information had on your preparation of the return.)		☐ Yes	☐ No	
5	Did you satisfy the record retention requirement? To meet the record retention requirement, you must keep a copy of your documentation referenced in 4b, a copy of this Form 8867, a copy of any applicable worksheets, a record of how, when, and from whom the information used to prepare Form 8867 and any applicable worksheet(s) was obtained, and a copy of any document(s) provided by the taxpayer that you relied on to determine eligibility for the credit(s) and /or HOH filing status or to compute the amount of the credit(s)? List those documents, if any, that you relied on.		☒ Yes	☐ No	
6	Did you ask the taxpayer whether he/she could provide documentation to substantiate eligibility for the credit(s) and/or HOH filing status and the amount of any credit(s) claimed on the return if his/her return is selected for audit?		☒ Yes	☐ No	
7	Did you ask the taxpayer if any of these credits were disallowed or reduced in a previous year?		☒ Yes	☐ No	☐ N/A
	(If credits were disallowed or reduced, go to question 7a; if not, go to question 8.)				
a	Did you complete the required recertification Form 8862?		☐ Yes	☐ No	☒ N/A
8	If the taxpayer is reporting self-employment income, did you ask questions to prepare a complete and correct Form 1040, Schedule C?		☐ Yes	☐ No	☒ N/A

For Paperwork Reduction Act Notice, see separate instructions.　　MXA　　F 11/12/18　　　　　　Form **8867** (2018)

Part II   Due Diligence Questions for Returns Claiming EIC (If the return does not claim EIC, go to Part III.)

	EIC	CTC/ ACTC/ODC	AOTC	HOH
9a Have you determined that this taxpayer is, in fact, eligible to claim the EIC for the number of children for whom the EIC is claimed, or to claim EIC if the taxpayer has no qualifying child? (Skip 9b and 9c if the taxpayer is claiming EIC and does not have a qualifying child.)	☒ Yes ☐ No			
b Did you ask the taxpayer if the child lived with the taxpayer for over half of the year, even if the taxpayer has supported the child for the entire year? . . .	☐ Yes ☐ No			
c Did you explain to the taxpayer the rules about claiming the EIC when a child is the qualifying child of more than one person (tie-breaker rules)?	☐ Yes ☐ No ☒ N/A			

Part III   Due Diligence Questions for Returns Claiming CTC/ACTC/ODC (if the return does not claim CTC or ACTC, or ODC go to Part IV.)

	EIC	CTC/ ACTC/ODC	AOTC	HOH
10 Have you determined that each qualifying person for the CTC/ACTC/ODC is the taxpayer's dependent who is a citizen, national, or resident of the United States?		☐ Yes ☐ No		
11 Did you explain to the taxpayer that he/she may not claim the CTC/ACTC if the taxpayer has not lived with the child for over half of the year, even if the taxpayer has supported the child, unless the child's custodial parent has released a claim to exemption for the child?		☐ Yes ☐ No ☐ N/A		
12 Did you explain to the taxpayer the rules about claiming the CTC/ACTC/ODC for a child of divorced or separated parents (or parents who live apart), including any requirement to attach a Form 8332 or similar statement to the return? . . .		☐ Yes ☐ No ☐ N/A		

Part IV   Due Diligence Questions for Returns Claiming AOTC (If return does not claim AOTC, go to Part V.)

	EIC	CTC/ ACTC/ODC	AOTC	HOH
13 Did the taxpayer provide the required substantiation for the credit, including a Form 1098-T and/or receipts for the qualified tuition and related expenses for the claimed AOTC?			☐ Yes ☐ No	

Part V   Due Diligence Questions for Returns Claiming HOH (If return does not claim HOH filing status, go to Part VI.)

	EIC	CTC/ ACTC/ODC	AOTC	HOH
14 Have you determined that the taxpayer was unmarried or considered unmarried on the last day of the tax year and provided more than half of the cost of keeping up a home for the year for a qualifying person?				☐ Yes ☐ No

Part VI   Eligiblity Certification

► **You will have complied with all due diligence requirments for claiming the applicable credit(s) and/or HOH filing status on the return of the taxpayer identified above if you:**

  A. Interview the taxpayer, ask adequate questions, document the taxpayer's responses on the return or in your notes, review adequate information to determine if the taxpayer is eligible to claim the credit(s) and/or HOH filing status and to determine the amount of the credit(s) claimed;

  B. Complete this Form 8867 truthfully and accurately and complete the actions described in this checklist for any applicable credit(s) claimed and HOH filing status, if claimed;

  C. Submit Form 8867 in the manner required; and

  D. Keep all five of the following records for 3 years from the latest dates specified in the Form 8867 instructions under *Document Retention*

    1. A copy of Form 8867;

    2. The applicable worksheet(s) or your own worksheet(s) for any credits claimed;

    3. Copies of any documents provided by the taxpayer on which you relied to determine eligibility for the credit(s) and/or HOH filing status;

    4. A record of how, when and from whom the information used to prepare this form and the applicable worksheet(s) was obtained; and

    5. A record of any additional questions you may have asked to determine eligibility to claim the credits, and/or HOH filing status and the amount(s) of any credit(s) claimed and the taxpayer's answers.

► **If you have not complied with all due diligence requirements, you may have to pay a $520 penalty for each failure to comply related to a claim of an applicable credit or HOH filing status.**

15 Do you certify that all of the answers on this Form 8867 are, to the best of your knowledge, true, correct and complete?	☒ Yes	☐ No

Form **8962**

Department of the Treasury
Internal Revenue Service

Premium Tax Credit (PTC)

▶ Attach to Form 1040, 1040A, or 1040NR.
▶ Go to www.irs.gov/Form8962 for instructions and the latest information.

OMB No. 1545-0074

2018

Attachment
Sequence No. **73**

Name shown on your return	Your social security number
HUSSEIN MUKHTAR T & SHARISH KHANDIA ABDULHUSAIN	617-75-5679

You cannot take the PTC if your filing status is married filing separately unless you are eligible for an exception (see instructions). If you qualify, check the box. ☐

Part I Annual and Monthly Contribution Amount

1	Tax family size. Enter your tax family size (see instructions)	**1**		**2**
2a	Modified AGI. Enter your modified AGI (see instructions)	**2a**	11,000	
b	Enter total of your dependents' modified AGI (see instructions)	**2b**		
3	Household income. Add the amounts on lines 2a and 2b. (see instructions)	**3**		**11,000**
4	Federal poverty line. Enter the federal poverty line amount from Table 1-1, 1-2, or 1-3 (see instructions). Check the appropriate box for the federal poverty table used. a ☐ Alaska b ☐ Hawaii c ☒ Other 48 states and DC	**4**		**16,240**
5	Household income as a percentage of federal poverty line (see instructions)	**5**		**67** %
6	Did you enter 401% on line 5? (see instructions if you entered less than 100%.)			
	☐ No. Continue to line 7.			
	☒ Yes. You are not eligible to receive PTC. If advance payment of PTC was made, see instructions for how to report your excess advance PTC repayment amount.			
7	Applicable Figure. Using your line 5 percentage, locate your "applicable figure" on the table in the instructions	**7**		
8a	Annual contribution amount. Multiply line 3 by line 7. Round to nearest whole dollar amount	**8a**	**b** Monthly contribution amount. Divide line 8a by 12. Round to nearest whole dollar amount	**8b**

Part II Premium Tax Credit Claim and Reconcilliation of Advance Payment of Premium Tax Credit

9 Are you allocating policy amounts with another taxpayer or do you want to use the alternative calculation for year of marriage (see instructions)?

☐ Yes. Skip to Part IV, Shared Policy Allocation, or Part V, Alternative Calculation for Year of Marriage. ☒ No. Continue to line 10.

10 See the instructions to determine if you can use line 11 or must complete lines 12 through 23.

☐ Yes. Continue to line 11. Compute your annual PTC. Then skip lines 12-23 and continue to line 24.

☒ No. Continue to lines 12-23. Compute your monthly PTC and continue to line 24.

Annual Calculation	(a) Annual enrollment premiums (Form(s) 1095-A, line 33A)	(b) Annual applicable SLCSP premium (Form(s) 1095-A, line 33B)	(c) Annual contribution amount (Line 8a)	(d) Annual maximum premium assistance (subtract (c) from (b), if zero or less, enter 0)	(e) Annual premium tax credit allowed (smaller of (a) or (d))	(f) Annual advance payment of PTC (Form(s) 1095-A, line 33C)
11 Annual Totals						

Monthly Calculation	(a) Monthly enrollment premiums (Form(s) 1095-A, lines 21-32, column A)	(b) Monthly applicable SLCSP premium (Form (s) 1095-A, lines 21-32 column B)	(c) Monthly contribution amount (amount from line 8b or alternative marriage monthly contribution)	(d) Monthly maximum premium assistance (subtract (c) from (b), if zero or less, enter 0)	(e) Monthly premium tax credit allowed (smaller of (a) or (d))	(f) Monthly advance payment of PTC (Form(s) 1095-A, lines 21 - 32, column C)
12 January						
13 February						
14 March						563
15 April						563
16 May						563
17 June						563
18 July						563
19 August						563
20 September						563
21 October						563
22 November						563
23 December						563

24	Total premium tax credit. Enter the amount from line 11(e) or add lines 12(e) through 23(e) and enter the total here	**24**	
25	Advance payment of PTC. Enter the amount from line 11(f) or add lines 12(f) through 23(f) and enter the total here.	**25**	**5,630**
26	Net premium tax credit. If line 24 is greater than line 25, subtract line 25 from line 24. Enter the difference here and on Schedule 5 (Form 1040), line 70, or Form 1040NR, line 65. If line 24 equals line 25, enter -0-. Stop here. If line 25 is greater than line 24, leave this line blank and continue to line 27.	**26**	

Part III Repayment of Excess Advance Payment of the Premium Tax Credit

27	Excess advance payment of PTC: If line 25 is greater than line 24, subtract line 24 from line 25. Enter the difference here. .	**27**	**5,630**
28	Repayment limitation: (see instructions)	**28**	**600**
29	Excess advance premium tax credit repayment: Enter the smaller of line 27 or line 28 here and on Schedule 2 (Form 1040), line 46, or Form 1040NR, line 44	**29**	**600**

For Paperwork Reduction Act Notice, see separate instructions.

Form **8962** (2018)

F 12/1/18

2018 California Resident Income Tax Return

FORM

540

APE   DO NOT ATTACH FEDERAL RETURN

18

A
R
RP

617-75-5679   ABDU   730-18-6921
HUSSEIN MUK   T   ABDULHUSAIN
SHARISH KHA   ABDULHUSAIN

2447 W ORANGE AVE
ANAHEIM   CA   92804

08-10-1989   10-24-1987

Filing Status

If your California filing status is different from your federal filing status, check the box here . . . . ☐

1 ☐ Single

4 ☐ Head of household (with qualifying person). See instructions.

2 ☒ Married/RDP filing jointly. See instructions.

5 ☐ Qualifying widow(er). Enter year spouse/RDP died ☐

See instructions.

3 ☐ Married/RDP filing separately. Enter spouse's/RDP's SSN or ITIN above and full name here ☐

6 If someone can claim you (or your spouse/RDP) as a dependent, fill in the box here. See instructions . . . . . . ● 6 ☐

▶ For line 7, line 8, line 9, and line 10: Multiply the amount you enter in the box by the pre-printed dollar amount for that line. **Whole dollars only**

Exemptions

7 **Personal:** If you checked box 1, 3, or 4 above, enter 1 in the box. If you checked box 2 or 5, enter 2 in the box. If you checked the box on line 6, see instructions . . . . ● 7 |2| X $118= ● $ |236.|

8 **Blind:** If you (or your spouse/RDP) are visually impaired, enter 1; if both are visually impaired, enter 2 . . . . ● 8 | | X $118= ● $ | |

9 **Senior:** If you (or your spouse/RDP) are 65 or older, enter 1; if both are 65 or older, enter 2 . . ● 9 | | X $118= ● $ | |

10 **Dependents:** Do not include yourself or your spouse/RDP.

	Dependent 1	Dependent 2	Dependent 3
First name ●		●	●
Last name ●		●	●
SSN ●		●	●
Dependent's relationship to you ●		●	●

Total dependent exemptions . . . . ● 10 | | X $367= ● $ | |

11 **Exemption amount:** Add line 7 through line 10. Transfer this amount to line 32 . . . . ● 11 $ |236.|

---

053   3101184   Form 540 2018   Side 1

Your name: HUSSEIN MUKHTAR T & SHARISH K Your SSN or ITIN: 617-75-5679

	12	State wages from your Form(s) W-2, box 16	● 12	11,000
Taxable income	13	Enter federal adjusted gross income from Form 1040, line 7	⊙ 13	11,000
	14	California adjustments - subtractions. Enter the amount from Schedule CA (540), line 37, column B	● 14	
	15	Subtract line 14 from line 13. If less than zero, enter the result in parentheses. See instructions.	15	11,000
	16	California adjustments - additions. Enter the amount from Schedule CA (540), line 37, column C	● 16	
	17	California adjusted gross income. Combine line 15 and line 16	● 17	11,000

18 Enter the larger of:
Your California **itemized deductions** from Schedule CA (540),Part II, line 30; OR
Your California **standard deduction** shown below for your filing status:
- Single or Married/RDP filing separately. $4,401
- Married/RDP filing jointly, Head of household, or Qualifying widow(er). $8,802   ● 18   8,802
- If Married/RDP filing separately or the box on line 6 is checked, STOP. See instructions.

	19	Subtract line 18 from line 17. This is your **taxable income**. If less than zero, enter -0-	⊙ 19	2,198

Tax	31	Tax. Check the box if from: [X] Tax Table [ ] Tax Rate Schedule ●[ ] FTB 3800 ●[ ] FTB 3803	● 31	22
	32	Exemption credits. Enter the amount from line 11. If your federal AGI is more than $194,504, see instructions.	⊙ 32	236
	33	Subtract line 32 from line 31. If less than zero, enter -0-	⊙ 33	0
	34	Tax. See instructions . Check the box if from ●[ ] Schedule G-1 ●[ ] FTB 5870A	● 34	0
	35	Add line 33 and line 34	⊙ 35	0

Special Credits	40	Nonrefundable Child and Dependent Care Expenses Credit. See instructions.	● 40	0
	43	Enter credit name [ ] code ●[ ] and amount	● 43	0
	44	Enter credit name [ ] code ●[ ] and amount	● 44	0
	45	To claim more than two credits, see instructions. Attach Schedule P (540)	● 45	
	46	Nonrefundable renter's credit. See instructions.	● 46	
	47	Add line 40 through line 46. These are your total credits	⊙ 47	
	48	Subtract line 47 from line 35. If less than zero, enter -0-.	⊙ 48	0

Other taxes	61	Alternative minimum tax. Attach Schedule P (540)	● 61	0
	62	Mental Health Services Tax. See instructions.	● 62	
	63	Other taxes and credit recapture. See instructions.	● 63	0
	64	Add line 48, line 61, line 62, and line 63. This is your total tax	● 64	0

Side 2   Form 540 2018   053   3102184

Your name: HUSSEIN MUKHTAR T & SHARISH   Your SSN or ITIN: 617-75-5679

71	California income tax withheld. See instructions.	● 71	103
72	2018 CA estimated tax and other payments. See instructions.	● 72	
73	Withholding (Form 592-B and/or 593). See instructions.	● 73	
74	Excess SDI (or VPDI) withheld. See instructions.	● 74	
75	Earned Income Tax Credit (EITC).	● 75	53
76	Add lines 71 through 75. These are your total payments. See instructions.	⊙76	156

91 Use Tax. Do not leave blank. See instructions . . . . 91 [0]

If line 91 is zero, check if: [X] No use tax is owed. ●

[ ] You paid your use tax obligation directly to CDTFA.

92	Payments balance. If line 76 is more than line 91, subtract line 91 from line 76.	92	156
93	Use Tax balance. If line 91 is more than line 76, subtract line 76 from line 91	⊙93 ⊙	
94	Overpaid tax. If line 92 is more than line 64, subtract line 64 from line 92.	94 ⊙	156
95	Amount of line 94 you want applied to your 2019 estimated tax.	● 95	
96	Overpaid tax available this year. Subtract line 95 from line 94.	● 96	156
97	Tax due. If line 92 is less than line 64, subtract line 92 from line 64.	⊙97	0

	Code	Amount
California Seniors Special Fund. See instructions	● 400	
Alzheimer's Disease and Related Dementia Voluntary Tax Contribution Fund	● 401	
Rare and Endangered Species Preservation Voluntary Tax Contribution Program	● 403	

Your name: HUSSEIN MUKHTAR T & SHARISH   Your SSN or ITIN: 617-75-5679

	Code	Amount
California Breast Cancer Research Voluntary Tax Contribution Fund	● 405	___ .00
California Firefighters' Memorial Fund	● 406	___ .00
Emergency Food For Families Voluntary Tax Contribution Fund	● 407	___ .00
California Peace Officer Memorial Foundation Fund	● 408	___ .00
California Sea Otter Fund	● 410	___ .00
California Cancer Research Voluntary Tax Contribution Fund	● 413	___ .00
School Supplies for Homeless Children Fund	● 422	___ .00
State Parks Protection Fund/Parks Pass Purchase	● 423	___ .00
Protect Our Coast and Oceans Voluntary Tax Contribution Fund	● 424	___ .00
Keep Arts in Schools Voluntary Tax Contribution Fund	● 425	___ .00
State Children's Trust Fund for the Prevention of Child Abuse	● 430	___ .00
Prevention of Animal Homelessness and Cruelty Fund	● 431	___ .00
Revive the Salton Sea Fund	● 432	___ .00
California Domestic Violence Victims Fund	● 433	___ .00
Special Olympics Fund	● 434	___ .00
Type 1 Diabetes Research Fund	● 435	___ .00
California YMCA Youth and Government Voluntary Tax Contribution Fund	● 436	___ .00
Habitat for Humanity Voluntary Tax Contribution Fund	● 437	___ .00
California Senior Citizen Advocacy Voluntary Tax Contribution Fund	● 438	___ .00
Native California Wildlife Rehabilitation Voluntary Tax Contribution Fund	● 439	___ .00
Rape Backlog Kit Voluntary Tax Contribution Fund	● 440	___ .00
Organ and Tissue Donor Registry Voluntary Tax Contribution Fund	● 441	___ .00
National Alliance on Mental Illness California Voluntary Tax Contribution Fund	● 442	___ .00
Schools Not Prisons Voluntary Tax Contribution Fund	● 443	___ .00
110 Add code 400 through code 443. This is your total contribution	● 110	0 .00

Contributions

Your name: HUSSEIN MUKHTAR T & SHARISH   Your SSN or ITIN: 617-75-5679

Amount You Owe

111 AMOUNT YOU OWE. If you do not have an amount on line 96, add line 93, line 97, and line 110. See instructions. **Do not send cash.**
Mail to: FRANCHISE TAX BOARD
PO BOX 942867
SACRAMENTO CA 94267-0001 . . . . ● 111 | 0 |.
Pay online - Go to ftb.ca.gov/pay for more information.

Interest and Penalties

112 Interest, late return penalties, and late payment penalties . . . . 112 | |.

113 Underpayment of estimated tax. Check the box: ● ☐ FTB 5805 attached ● ☐ FTB 5805F attached ● 113 | |.

114 Total amount due. See instructions. Enclose, but **do not staple**, any payment . . . . 114 | |.

115 REFUND OR NO AMOUNT DUE. Subtract the sum of line 110, line 112 and line 113 from line 96. See instructions.
Mail to: FRANCHISE TAX BOARD
PO BOX 942840
SACRAMENTO CA 94240-0001 . . . . ● 115 | 156 |.

Direct Deposit

Fill in the information to authorize direct deposit of your refund into one or two accounts. Do not attach a voided check or a deposit slip. See instructions.
Have you verified the routing and account numbers? Use whole dollars only.
All or the following amount of my refund (line 115) is authorized for direct deposit into the account shown below:

● Type
☒ Checking

● Routing number   ● Account number
| 121000358 | ☐ Savings | ********8506 | ● 116 Direct deposit amount | 156 |.

The remaining amount of my refund (line 115) is authorized for direct deposit into the account shown below:

● Type
☐ Checking

● Routing number   ● Account number
| | ☐ Savings | | ● 117 Direct deposit amount | |.

IMPORTANT: See the instructions to find out if you should attach a copy of your complete federal tax return.

To learn about your privacy rights, how we may use your information, and the consequences for not providing the requested information, go to ftb.ca.gov/forms and search for 1131. To request this notice by mail, call 800.852.5711. Under penalties of perjury, I declare that I have examined this tax return, including accompanying schedules and statements, and to the best of my knowledge and belief, it is true, correct, and complete.

Your signature   Date   Spouse's/RDP's signature (if a joint tax return, both must sign)

Sign Here

It is unlawful to forge a spouse's/RDP's signature.

Joint tax return? (See instructions)

● Your email address. Enter only one email address.   ● Preferred phone number
HUSSAINMUKHTAR@GMAIL.COM

Paid preparer's signature (declaration of preparer is based on all information of which preparer has any knowledge)

Firm's name (or yours, if self-employed)   ● PTIN
                                                   P02145227

Firm's address   ● Firm's FEIN
JACKSON HEWITT TAX SERVICE
11822 GILBERT ST   GARDEN GROVE, CA 92841   22-3677427

Do you want to allow another person to discuss this return with us? See instructions. . . . . ● ☒ Yes ● ☐ No
Print Third Party Designee's Name   Telephone Number
TONYA BIXLER   (562) 506-1009

F 12/18/18   053   3105184   Form 540 2018   Side 5

TAXABLE YEAR

FORM

2018   **California Earned Income Tax Credit**   **3514**

Attach to your California Form 540, Form 540 2EZ or Long or Short Form 540NR

Name(s) as shown on tax return

SSN

HUSSEIN MUKHTAR T & SHARISH KHANDIA ABDULHUSAIN   617-75-5679

Before you begin:

If you claim the EITC even though you know you are not eligible, you may not be allowed to take the credit for up to 10 years.

Follow Step 1 through Step 7 in the instructions to determine if you meet the requirements, to complete this form, and to figure the amount of the credit.

If you are claiming the California Earned Income Tax Credit (EITC), you must provide your date of birth (DOB), and spouse's/RDP's DOB if filing jointly, on your California Form 540, Form 540 2EZ, or Long or Short Form 540NR.

Part I   Qualifying Information   See Specific Instructions.

1 a Has the Internal Revenue Service (IRS) previously disallowed your federal Earned Income Credit (EIC)?........ ◉ ☐ Yes ☒ No

   b Has the Franchise Tax Board (FTB) previously disallowed your California EITC?. . . . . ◉ ☐ Yes ☒ No

2 Federal AGI (federal Form 1040, line 7) . . . . ● 2   11,000

3 Federal EIC (federal Form 1040, line 17a). . . . . ● 3   519

Part II   Investment Income Information

4 Investment Income. See instructions for Step 2 - Investment Income. ● 4   0

Part III   Qualifying Child Information

You must complete Part I and Part II before filling out Part III. If you are not claiming a qualifying child, skip Part III and go to Step 4 in the instructions.

Qualifying Child Information	Child 1	Child 2	Child 3
5 First Name . . . . ◉		◉	◉
6 Last Name . . . . ◉		◉	◉
7 SSN . . . . ●		●	●
8 Date of Birth (mm/dd/yyyy). If born after 1999 and the child is younger than you (or your spouse/RDP, if filing jointly), skip line 9a and line 9b; go to line 10 ◉		◉	◉

9 a Was the child under age 24 at the end of 2018, a student, and younger than you (or your spouse/ RDP, if filing jointly)? If yes, go to line 10. If no, go to line 9b. See instructions. . . . . ◉ ☐ Yes ☐ No   ◉ ☐ Yes ☐ No   ◉ ☐ Yes ☐ No

   b Was the child permanently and totally disabled during any part of 2018? If yes, go to line 10 . If no, stop here . The child is not a qualifying child . ◉ ☐ Yes ☐ No   ◉ ☐ Yes ☐ No   ◉ ☐ Yes ☐ No

10 Child's relationship to you See instructions. . . . . ◉   ◉   ◉

11 Number of days child lived with you in California during 2018. Do not enter more than 365 days. See instructions. . . ◉   ◉   ◉

		Child 1	Child 2	Child 3

12 a Child's physical address during 2018 (number, street, and apt. no./ste. no). See instructions

b City

c State

d ZIP Code

Part IV California Earned Income

13	Wages, salaries, tips, and other employee compensation, subject to California withholding. See instructions	● 13	11,000
14	IHSS payments. See instructions.	⊙ 14	
15	Prison Inmate wages and/or pension or annuity from a nonqualified deferred compensation plan or a nongovernmental IRC Section 457 plan. See instructions.	⊙ 15	
16	Subtract Line 14 and 15 from line 13.	● 16	11,000
17	Nontaxable combat pay. See instructions	⊙ 17	

18 Business income or (loss). Enter amount from Worksheet 3, line 5. See instructions . . . . ⊙ 18

    a Business name . . . . ⊙

    b Business address . . . . ⊙

       City, state and zip code . . . . ⊙

    c Business license number . . . ⊙

    d SEIN . . . . ⊙

    e Business code . . . . ⊙

19	**California Earned Income.** Add line 16, line 17, and line 18	● 19	11,000

Part V California Earned Income Tax Credit (Complete Step 6 in the instructions.)

20	California EITC. Enter amount from California Earned Income Tax Credit Worksheet, Part III, line 6.. This amount should also be entered on Form 540, line 75 or Form 540 EZ, Line 23.	● 20	53

Part VI Nonresident or Part-Year Resident California Earned Income Tax Credit

21	CA Exemption Credit Percentage from Form 540NR (Long or Short), line 38 ⊙ 21	
22	**Nonresident or Part-Year Resident EITC.** Multiply line 20 by line 21. This amount should also be entered on Form 540NR (Long or Short), line 85. . . . . ● 22	

Paid Preparer's California
Earned Income Tax Credit Checklist

FORM
3596

Attach to taxpayer's original or amended California Form 540, Form 540 2EZ or Form 540NR (Long or Short)

Name(s) as shown on tax return

SSN or ITIN

HUSSEIN MUKHTAR T & SHARISH KHANDIA ABDULHUSAIN   617-75-5679

Part I - Due Diligence Requirements

1 a Preparer's name .... ⊙ 1a   THU LE

   b Preparer's PTIN .... ⊙ 1b   P02145227

   c Preparer's license, registration, or enrollment type. Check one box

      ☐ CPA   ☐ EA   ☐ Attorney   ☒ CTEC   ☐ Other (specify)

      If CPA, Attorney, or Other, enter license, registration, or enrollment state   ⊙ 1c

   d Preparer's license, registration, or enrollment number   ⊙ 1d   A303589

2 Did you complete form FTB 3514, California Earned Income Tax Credit (EITC), based on current
   information provided by the taxpayer or reasonably obtained by you? ....   2 ☒ Yes   ☐ No

3 Did you complete the California Earned Income Tax Credit Worksheet found in the form FTB 3514 instructions,
   or your own worksheet that provides the same information as the form FTB 3514 worksheet? ....   3 ☒ Yes   ☐ No

4 Did you satisfy the knowledge requirement? To meet the knowledge requirement, you must do both of the following:
   • Interview the taxpayer, ask questions, and document the taxpayer's responses to determine that the taxpayer
     is eligible to claim the EITC
   • Review information to determine that the taxpayer is eligible to claim the credit and for what amount ...   4 ☒ Yes   ☐ No

5 Did any information provided by the taxpayer, a third party, or reasonably known to you, in connection with
   preparing Form 3514 appear to be incorrect, incomplete, or inconsistent?
   (If "yes," answer questions 5a and 5b. If "no," go to question 6.) ....   5 ☐ Yes   ☒ No

   a Did you make reasonable inquiries to determine the correct, complete, and consistent information? ....   5a ☐ Yes   ☐ No

   b Did you document your inquiries? (Documentation should include the questions you asked, whom you asked,
      when you asked, the information that was provided, and the impact the information had on your preparation
      of form FTB 3514.) ....   5b ☐ Yes   ☐ No

6 Did you satisfy the record retention requirement? To meet the record retention requirement, you must keep a copy
   of your documentation referenced in 5b, a copy of this form, a copy of applicable worksheets, a record of how,
   when and from whom the information used to prepare form FTB 3514 and worksheet(s) was obtained, and a copy
   of any document(s) provided by the taxpayer that you relied on to determine eligibility or to compute the amount for
   the credit ....   6 ☒ Yes   ☐ No
   List those documents, if any, that you relied on.

   _____
   _____
   _____

7 Did you ask the taxpayer whether he/she could provide documentation to substantiate eligibility for and the amount
   of the EITC claimed on the return if his/her return is selected for audit? ....   7 ☒ Yes   ☐ No

8 If the taxpayer is reporting self-employment income, did you ask questions to prepare a complete and correct
   federal Form 1040, Schedule C, Schedule C-EZ, Schedule F, or Schedule SE? ....   8 ☐ Yes   ☐ No
                                                                                      ☒ N/A

Part II - Due Diligence Questions

9 a Have you determined that the taxpayer is, in fact, eligible to claim the EITC for the number of children whom the EITC is claimed, or to claim the EITC if the taxpayer has no qualifying child? (Skip 9b and 9c if the taxpayer is claiming EITC and does not have a qualifying child.) . . . . 9a ☒ Yes ☐ No

b Did you explain to the taxpayer that he/she may not claim the EITC if the taxpayer has not lived with the child for over half the year, even if the taxpayer has supported the child? . . . . 9b ☐ Yes ☐ No

c Did you explain to the taxpayer the rules about claiming the EITC when a child is the qualifying child of more than one person (tie-breaker rules)? . . . . 9c ☐ Yes ☐ No
☒ N/A

Part III - Credit Eligibility Certification

You have complied with all the due diligence requirements if you:

A. Interview the taxpayer, ask adequate questions, document the taxpayer's responses on the return or in your notes, review adequate information to determine if the taxpayer is eligible to claim the credit and in what amount; and
B. Complete this form FTB 3596 truthfully and accurately and complete the actions described in this checklist;
C. Submit form FTB 3596 in the manner required;
D. Keep all five of the following records for 4 years from the latest of the dates specified in the instructions under Document Retention:
   a. A copy of form FTB 3596,
   b. Submit form FTB 3596 in the manner required;
   c. Copies of any taxpayer documents you relied on to determine eligibility for or amount of EIC.
   d. A record of how, when, & from whom the information used to prepare the form and worksheet(s) was obtained, and
   e. A record of any additional questions you asked and your client's answers.

If you have not complied with all the due diligence requirements for the EITC claimed, you may have to pay a $500 penalty for each failure to comply.

10 Do you certify that all of the answers on this form FTB 3596 are, to the best of your knowledge, true, correct, and complete? . . . . 10 ☒ Yes ☐ No

LYFT, INC
185 BERRY ST. SUITE 5000
SAN FRANCISCO, CA 94107

Have questions? Visit the Lyft
Help Center for more information:
http://help.lyft.com

HUSSEIN ABDULHUSAIN
2447 W ORANGE AVE
ANAHEIM, CA 92804

	CORRECTED (if checked)		
FILER'S name, street address, city or town, state or province, country, ZIP or foreign postal code, and telephone no. LYFT, INC 185 BERRY ST. SUITE 5000 SAN FRANCISCO, CA 94107	FILER'S TIN 20-8809830	OMB No. 1545-2205	**Payment Card and Third Party Network Transactions**
	PAYEE'S TIN *****5679	**2019**	
	1a Gross amount of payment card/third party network transactions $23,165.12	Form 1099-K	

Check to indicate if FILER is a (an):		Check to indicate transactions reported are:		1b Card Not Present transactions	2 Merchant category code 4121	Copy B For Payee
Payment settlement entity (PSE)	X	Payment card		3 Number of payment transactions 1492	4 Federal income tax withheld	This is important tax information and is being furnished to the IRS. If you are required to file a return, a negligence penalty or other sanction may be imposed on you if taxable income results from this transaction and the IRS determines that it has not been reported.
Electronic Payment Facilitator (EPF)/Other third party		Third party network	X	5a January	5b February $848.06	
PAYEE'S name, street address, city or town, state or province, country, and ZIP or foreign postal code HUSSEIN ABDULHUSAIN 2447 W ORANGE AVE ANAHEIM, CA 92804				5c March $748.52	5d April $650.96	
				5e May $926.18	5f June $666.02	
				5g July $2,332.76	5h August $3,481.01	
PSE'S name and telephone number				5i September $3,190.82	5j October $3,206.75	
				5k November $3,796.50	5l December $3,317.54	
Account number (see instructions) 1079546304593986482				6 State CA	7 State identification no.	8 State income tax withheld

Form 1099-K   (keep for your records)   www.irs.gov/Form1099K   Department of the Treasury - Internal Revenue Service

1099-K Instructions for Payee

You have received this form because you have either (a) accepted payment cards for payments, or (b) received payments through a third party network that exceeded $20,000 in gross total reportable transactions and the aggregate number of those transactions exceeded 200 for the calendar year. Merchant acquirers and third party settlement organizations, as payment settlement entities (PSEs), must report the proceeds of payment card and third party network transactions made to you on Form 1099-K under Internal Revenue Code section 6050W. The PSE may have contracted with an electronic payment facilitator (EPF) or other third party payer to make payments to you.

If you have questions about the amounts reported on this form, contact the FILER whose information is shown in the upper left corner on the front of this form. If you do not recognize the FILER shown in the upper left corner of the form, contact the PSE whose name and phone number are shown in the lower left corner of the form above your account number.

See the separate instructions for your income tax return for using the information reported on this form.

Payee's taxpayer identification number (TIN). For your protection, this form may show only the last four digits of your TIN (social security number (SSN), individual taxpayer identification number (ITIN), adoption taxpayer identification number (ATIN), or employer identification number (EIN)). However, the issuer has reported your complete TIN to the IRS.

Account number. May show an account number or other unique number the PSE assigned to distinguish your account.

Box 1a. Shows the aggregate gross amount of payment card/third party network transactions made to you through the PSE during the calendar year.

Box 1b. Shows the aggregate gross amount of all reportable payment transactions made to you through the PSE during the calendar year where the card was not present at the time of the transaction or the card number was keyed into the terminal. Typically, this relates to online sales, phone sales, or catalogue sales. If the box for third party network is checked, or if these are third party network transactions, Card Not Present transactions will not be reported.

Box 2. Shows the merchant category code used for payment card/ third party network transactions (if available) reported on this form.

Box 3. Shows the number of payment transactions (not including refund transactions) processed through the payment card/third party network.

Box 4. Shows backup withholding. Generally, a payer must backup withhold if you did not furnish your TIN or you did not furnish the correct TIN to the payer. See Form W-9, Request for Taxpayer Identification Number and Certification, and Pub. 505. Include this amount on your income tax return as tax withheld.

Boxes 5a-5l. Shows the gross amount of payment card/third party network transactions made to you for each month of the calendar year.

Boxes 6-8. Shows state and local income tax withheld from the payments.

Future developments. For the latest information about developments related to Form 1099-K and its instructions, such as legislation enacted after they were published, go to www.irs.gov/Form1099K

LYFT, INC
185 BERRY ST. SUITE 5000
SAN FRANCISCO, CA 94107

Have questions? Visit the Lyft
Help Center for more information:
http://help.lyft.com

HUSSEIN ABDULHUSAIN
2447 W ORANGE AVE
ANAHEIM, CA 92804

☐ CORRECTED (if checked)		

PAYER'S name, street address, city or town, state or province, country, ZIP or foreign postal code, and telephone no. LYFT, INC 185 BERRY ST. SUITE 5000 SAN FRANCISCO, CA 94107	1 Rents	OMB No. 1545-0115	
	2 Royalties	**2019**	**Miscellaneous Income**
	3 Other income	Form 1099-MISC	
PAYER'S TIN 20-8809830	RECIPIENT'S TIN *****5679	5 Fishing boat proceeds	4 Federal income tax withheld	**Copy B** **For Recipient**
			6 Medical and health care payments	This is important tax information and is being furnished to the IRS. If you are required to file a return, a negligence penalty or other sanction may be imposed on you if this income is taxable and the IRS determines that it has not been reported.
RECIPIENT'S name, street address, city or town, state or province, country, and ZIP or foreign postal code HUSSEIN ABDULHUSAIN 2447 W ORANGE AVE ANAHEIM, CA 92804	7 Nonemployee compensation $783.83	8 Substitute payments in lieu of dividends or interest	
	9 Payer made direct sales of $5,000 or more of consumer products to a buyer (recipient) for resale ☐	10 Crop insurance proceeds	
	11	12	
Account number (see instructions) 1079546304593986482	FATCA filing requirement ☐	13 Excess golden parachute payments	14 Gross proceeds paid to an attorney	
15a Section 409A deferrals	15b Section 409A income	16 State tax withheld	17 State/Payer's state no. CA	18 State income

Form **1099-MISC** (keep for your records) www.irs.gov/Form1099MISC Department of the Treasury - Internal Revenue Service

Uber

1455 Market St

San Francisco, CA 94103

Uber Tax ID Number: 45-3847441

Tax Summary for 2019

Thanks for doing driving with Uber in 2019. Below is a breakdown of your earnings over the year that may help you file your taxes.

Driving Totals	**2,241**	**24,022**
Online Miles shows all of the miles you drove while online, including off trip miles.	COMPLETED TRIPS	ONLINE MILES

Your Gross Earnings

Total Trip Earnings from Uber plus any other additional earnings

Gross Trip Earnings	+ $31,958.33
Total Additional Earnings	+ $278.33

$32,236.66

Expenses, Fees and Tax

Expenses, Fees and Tax. For a complete breakdown, please refer to table 1 on page 2.

Expenses, Fees and Tax	+ $10,778.12

$10,778.12

Your Net Payout

Not for tax filing purposes. This amount represents what was paid in your bank account.

Net Earnings	$21,333.07
Reimbursements: Tolls	+ $125.47

$21,458.54

Uber

1455 Market St

San Francisco, CA 94103

Uber Tax ID Number: 45-2647441

Tax Summary for 2019

Table 1 - Expenses, Fees, Tax and Reimbursement

All items marked with a * may be tax deductible. Your online mileage may also be deductible. Need help filing? Get help from the tax experts. Visit t.uber.com/turbotax or consult a tax professional for more information.

Expenses, Fees and Tax	
Uber service fee/other adjustments*	$4,737.92
Booking fee*	$6,036.20
Split fare fee*	$4.00
Airport and/or city fee paid by Uber or subsidiaries*	$759.05
Reimbursements	
Tolls, airport fees and surcharges*	$125.47
TOTAL EXPENSES, FEES, TAX AND REIMBURSEMENTS	**$10,903.59**

"Uber Service Fee / Other Adjustments" includes both the Uber Service Fee and certain other items such as 1) pricing adjustments due to Uber-provided rider promotions, or 2) differences between the rider's upfront price and your earnings.

Table - 2 Additional Payments from Uber or Subsidiaries

Incentives*	$278.33
TOTAL ADDITIONAL EARNINGS	**$278.33**

This is not an official tax document. Uber does not offer any tax advice.

Check with a tax professional or go to t.uber.com/taxes-faq for more information.

2019 summary

lyft

Hussein Abdulhusain

Here's a summary of your earnings and rides for 2019. Thanks for driving with Lyft!

If you received over $20,000 in gross ride earnings you will also receive a 1099-K by January, 31st 2020
If you received over $600 in non-ride related earnings you will also receive a 1099-M by January 31st, 2020

Your driving totals	**1479**	**18537.13**
	Rides	Online miles

Gross earnings

Ride payments	$23,165.12
Non-ride earnings	$783.83

Expenses

Lyft platform fees	$5,164.75
Service fees	$4,003.66
Third-party fees	$561.15
Tolls	$52.99

Online miles

The total miles you drove while online, including miles when you weren't picking up or dropping off a passenger.

Ride payments

The total amount passengers paid for the rides you gave including: tips from passengers, third party fees, and other expenses.

Non-ride earnings

The total amount you earned outside of the rides you gave (like bonuses or referrals).

Lyft platform fees

The total Lyft platform fees passengers paid for the rides you gave. We use platform fees to help maintain the Lyft business.

Service fees

The total service fees passengers paid for the rides you gave. Service fees are added to every ride to support some of Lyft's operational costs, like insurance and background checks.

Third-party fees

The total third-party fees passengers paid for the rides you gave. Third-party fees include things like airport fees or local taxes.

Tolls

The total tolls passengers paid for the rides you gave.

3 Social security wages	2100.60	4 Social security tax withheld	89.11
	2100.60		130.24
5 Medicare wages and tips	2100.60	6 Medicare tax withheld	30.46

c Employer's name, address, and ZIP code

COWORX STAFFING SERVICES LLC
412 MOUNT KEMBLE AVE
SUITE 200C
MORRISTOWN, NJ 07960

7 Social security tips	8 Allocated tips	9
10 Dependent care benefits	11 Nonqualified plans	12a See instructions for box 12
12b	12c	12d
12e	b Employer identification number (EIN) 22-3722243	a Employee's social security number 730-18-6921

13 Statutory employee	Retirement plan	Third-party sick pay	14 Other
☐	☐	☐	

e/f Employee's name, address, and ZIP code

SHARISH K ABDULHUSAIN
2447 W ORANGE AVE
ANAHEIM, CA 92804-3447

Import Code: BSXU8QZM

Form W-2	15 State CA	Employer's state ID number 37263506	16 State wages, tips, etc. 2100.60
Wage and Tax Statement	17 State income tax 15.67		18 Local wages, tips, etc. 2100.60
2019	19 Local income tax 21.01		20 Locality name CA SDI

Copy C - For EMPLOYEE'S RECORDS (See Notice to Employee on the back of Copy 2.)

---

3 Social security wages	2100.60	4 Social security tax withheld	89.11
	2100.60		130.24
5 Medicare wages and tips	2100.60	6 Medicare tax withheld	30.46

c Employer's name, address, and ZIP code

COWORX STAFFING SERVICES LLC
412 MOUNT KEMBLE AVE
SUITE 200C
MORRISTOWN, NJ 07960

7 Social security tips	8 Allocated tips	9
10 Dependent care benefits	11 Nonqualified plans	12a
12b	12c	12d
12e	b Employer identification number (EIN) 22-3722243	a Employee's social security number 730-18-6921

13 Statutory employee	Retirement plan	Third-party sick pay	14 Other
☐	☐	☐	

e/f Employee's name, address, and ZIP code

SHARISH K ABDULHUSAIN
2447 W ORANGE AVE
ANAHEIM, CA 92804-3447

Import Code: BSXU8QZM

Form W-2	15 State CA	Employer's state ID number 37263506	16 State wages, tips, etc. 2100.60
Wage and Tax Statement	17 State income tax 15.67		18 Local wages, tips, etc. 2100.60
2019	19 Local income tax 21.01		20 Locality name CA SDI

Copy 2 - To Be Filed With Employee's State, City, or Local Income Tax Return.

OMB No. 1545-0008 Department of the Treasury - Internal Revenue Service

d Control number	1 Wages, tips, other compensation 2100.60	2 Federal income tax withheld 89.11
This information is being furnished to the	3 Social security wages 2100.60	4 Social security tax withheld 130.24
Internal Revenue Service.	5 Medicare wages and tips 2100.60	6 Medicare tax withheld 30.46

e Employer's name, address, and ZIP code

COWORX STAFFING SERVICES LLC
412 MOUNT KEMBLE AVE
SUITE 200C
MORRISTOWN, NJ 07960

7 Social security tips	8 Allocated tips	9
10 Dependent care benefits	11 Nonqualified plans	12a See instructions for box 12
12b	12c	12d
12e	b Employer identification number (EIN) 22-3722243	a Employee's social security number 730-18-6921

13 Statutory employee	Retirement plan	Third-party sick pay	14 Other
☐	☐	☐	

e/f Employee's name, address, and ZIP code

SHARISH K ABDULHUSAIN
2447 W ORANGE AVE
ANAHEIM, CA 92804-3447

Import Code: BSXU8QZM

Form W-2	15 State CA	Employer's state ID number 37263506	16 State wages, tips, etc. 2100.60
Wage and Tax Statement	17 State income tax 15.67		18 Local wages, tips, etc. 2100.60
2019	19 Local income tax 21.01		20 Locality name CA SDI

Copy B - To Be Filed With Employee's FEDERAL Tax Return.

OMB No. 1545-0008 Department of the Treasury - Internal Revenue Service

d Control number	1 Wages, tips, other compensation 2100.60	2 Federal income tax withheld 89.11
	3 Social security wages 2100.60	4 Social security tax withheld 130.24
	5 Medicare wages and tips 2100.60	6 Medicare tax withheld 30.46

e Employer's name, address, and ZIP code

COWORX STAFFING SERVICES LLC
412 MOUNT KEMBLE AVE
SUITE 200C
MORRISTOWN, NJ 07960

7 Social security tips	8 Allocated tips	9
10 Dependent care benefits	11 Nonqualified plans	12a
12b	12c	12d
12e	b Employer identification number (EIN) 22-3722243	a Employee's social security number 730-18-6921

13 Statutory employee	Retirement plan	Third-party sick pay	14 Other
☐	☐	☐	

e/f Employee's name, address, and ZIP code

SHARISH K ABDULHUSAIN
2447 W ORANGE AVE
ANAHEIM, CA 92804-3447

Import Code: BSXU8QZM

Form W-2	15 State CA	Employer's state ID number 37263506	16 State wages, tips, etc. 2100.60
Wage and Tax Statement	17 State income tax 15.67		18 Local wages, tips, etc. 2100.60
2019	19 Local income tax 21.01		20 Locality name CA SDI

Copy 2 - To Be Filed With Employee's State, City, or Local Income Tax Return.

Form 1040 Department of the Treasury—Internal Revenue Service (99)

U.S. Individual Income Tax Return | 2019 | OMB No. 1545-0074 | IRS Use Only—Do not write or staple in this space.

Filing Status
Check only one box.

☐ Single ☒ Married filing jointly ☐ Married filing separately (MFS) ☐ Head of household (HOH) ☐ Qualifying widow(er) (QW)

If you checked the MFS box, enter the name of spouse. If you checked the HOH or QW box, enter the child's name if the qualifying person is a child but not your dependent. ▶

Your first name and middle initial	Last name	Your social security number
Hussein M	Abdulhusain	617-75-5679
If joint return, spouse's first name and middle initial	Last name	Spouse's social security number
Sharish K	Abdulhusain	730-18-6921

Home address (number and street). If you have a P.O. box, see instructions. | Apt. no.

2447 W Orange Ave

City, town or post office, state, and ZIP code. If you have a foreign address, also complete spaces below (see instructions).

Anaheim CA 92804-3447

Presidential Election Campaign
Check here if you, or your spouse if filing jointly, want $3 to go to this fund. Checking a box below will not change your tax or refund. ☐ You ☐ Spouse

Foreign country name	Foreign province/state/county	Foreign postal code

If more than four dependents, see instructions and ✓ here ▶ ☐

Standard Deduction

Someone can claim: ☐ You as a dependent ☐ Your spouse as a dependent

☐ Spouse itemizes on a separate return or you were a dual-status alien

Age/Blindness You: ☐ Were born before January 2, 1955 ☐ Are blind Spouse: ☐ Was born before January 2, 1955 ☐ Is blind

Dependents (see instructions):

(1) First name Last name	(2) Social security number	(3) Relationship to you	(4) ✓ if qualifies for (see instructions): Child tax credit	Credit for other dependents
Ayaan H Abdulhusain	891-56-7642	Son	☒	☐
			☐	☐
			☐	☐
			☐	☐

Standard Deduction for—
- Single or Married filing separately, $12,200
- Married filing jointly or Qualifying widow(er), $24,400
- Head of household, $18,350
- If you checked any box under Standard Deduction, see instructions.

1	Wages, salaries, tips, etc. Attach Form(s) W-2			1	2,101.
2a	Tax-exempt interest	2a	b Taxable interest. Attach Sch. B if required	2b	
3a	Qualified dividends	3a	b Ordinary dividends. Attach Sch. B if required	3b	
4a	IRA distributions	4a	b Taxable amount	4b	
c	Pensions and annuities	4c	d Taxable amount	4d	
5a	Social security benefits	5a	b Taxable amount	5b	
6	Capital gain or (loss). Attach Schedule D if required. If not required, check here ▶ ☐			6	
7a	Other income from Schedule 1, line 9			7a	5,944.
b	Add lines 1, 2b, 3b, 4b, 4d, 5b, 6, and 7a. This is your **total income** ▶			7b	8,045.
8a	Adjustments to income from Schedule 1, line 22			8a	1,843.
b	Subtract line 8a from line 7b. This is your **adjusted gross income** ▶			8b	6,202.
9	Standard deduction or itemized deductions (from Schedule A)		9	24,400.	
10	Qualified business income deduction. Attach Form 8995 or Form 8995-A		10	0.	
11a	Add lines 9 and 10			11a	24,400.
b	**Taxable income.** Subtract line 11a from line 8b. If zero or less, enter -0-			11b	0.

For Disclosure, Privacy Act, and Paperwork Reduction Act Notice, see separate instructions.

Form **1040** (2019)

	12a	Tax (see inst.) Check if any from Form(s): 1 ☐ 8814 2 ☐ 4972 3 ☐ _____	12a	0.			
	b	Add Schedule 2, line 3, and line 12a and enter the total ▶			12b		0.
	13a	Child tax credit or credit for other dependents	13a	0.			
	b	Add Schedule 3, line 7, and line 13a and enter the total ▶			13b		0.
	14	Subtract line 13b from line 12b. If zero or less, enter -0-			14		0.
	15	Other taxes, including self-employment tax, from Schedule 2, line 10			15		840.
	16	Add lines 14 and 15. This is your **total tax** ▶			16		840.
	17	Federal income tax withheld from Forms W-2 and 1099			17		89.
• If you have a qualifying child, attach Sch. EIC.	18	Other payments and refundable credits:					
	a	Earned income credit (EIC)	18a	2,593.			
• If you have nontaxable combat pay, see instructions.	b	Additional child tax credit. Attach Schedule 8812	18b	769.			
	c	American opportunity credit from Form 8863, line 8	18c				
	d	Schedule 3, line 14	18d	1,596.			
	e	Add lines 18a through 18d. These are your **total other payments and refundable credits** ▶			18e		4,958.
	19	Add lines 17 and 18e. These are your **total payments** ▶			19		5,047.
Refund	20	If line 19 is more than line 16, subtract line 16 from line 19. This is the amount you **overpaid**			20		4,207.
	21a	Amount of line 20 you want **refunded to you.** If Form 8888 is attached, check here ▶ ☐			21a		4,207.
Direct deposit? See instructions.	▶ b	Routing number 1 2 1 0 0 0 3 5 8 ▶ c Type: ☒ Checking ☐ Savings					
	▶ d	Account number 0 0 2 3 4 5 6 6 8 5 0 6					
	22	Amount of line 20 you want applied to your **2020 estimated tax** ▶	22				
Amount You Owe	23	**Amount you owe.** Subtract line 19 from line 16. For details on how to pay, see instructions ▶			23		
	24	Estimated tax penalty (see instructions) ▶	24				

Third Party Designee

(Other than paid preparer)

Do you want to allow another person (other than your paid preparer) to discuss this return with the IRS? See instructions.   ☐ **Yes.** Complete below.   ☒ **No**

Designee's name ▶	Phone no. ▶	Personal identification number (PIN) ▶	

Sign Here

Joint return? See instructions. Keep a copy for your records.

Under penalties of perjury, I declare that I have examined this return and accompanying schedules and statements, and to the best of my knowledge and belief, they are true, correct, and complete. Declaration of preparer (other than taxpayer) is based on all information of which preparer has any knowledge.

Your signature	Date	Your occupation	If the IRS sent you an Identity Protection PIN, enter it here (see inst.)	
		Driver		
Spouse's signature. If a joint return, **both** must sign.	Date	Spouse's occupation	If the IRS sent your spouse an Identity Protection PIN, enter it here (see inst.)	
		Homemaker		
Phone no.		Email address		

Paid Preparer Use Only

Preparer's name	Preparer's signature	Date	PTIN	Check if:
				☐ 3rd Party Designee
Firm's name ▶ Self-Prepared		Phone no.		☐ Self-employed
Firm's address ▶			Firm's EIN ▶	

Go to *www.irs.gov/Form1040* for instructions and the latest information.   **BAA**   REV 03 08 20 Intuit.cg.cfp.sp   Form **1040** (2019)

SCHEDULE 1
(Form 1040 or 1040-SR)

Department of the Treasury
Internal Revenue Service

Additional Income and Adjustments to Income

► Attach to Form 1040 or 1040-SR.
► Go to *www.irs.gov/Form1040* for instructions and the latest information.

OMB No. 1545-0074

2019

Attachment
Sequence No. 01

Name(s) shown on Form 1040 or 1040-SR	Your social security number
Hussein M & Sharish K Abdulhusain	617-75-5679

At any time during 2019, did you receive, sell, send, exchange, or otherwise acquire any financial interest in any virtual currency? . . . . ☐ Yes ☒ No

Part I	Additional Income		
1	Taxable refunds, credits, or offsets of state and local income taxes	1	
2a	Alimony received	2a	
b	Date of original divorce or separation agreement (see instructions) ► _____		
3	Business income or (loss). Attach Schedule C	3	5,944.
4	Other gains or (losses). Attach Form 4797	4	
5	Rental real estate, royalties, partnerships, S corporations, trusts, etc. Attach Schedule E . . .	5	
6	Farm income or (loss). Attach Schedule F	6	
7	Unemployment compensation	7	
8	Other income. List type and amount ► _____		
		8	
9	Combine lines 1 through 8. Enter here and on Form 1040 or 1040-SR, line 7a	9	5,944.
Part II	Adjustments to Income		
10	Educator expenses	10	
11	Certain business expenses of reservists, performing artists, and fee-basis government officials. Attach Form 2106	11	
12	Health savings account deduction. Attach Form 8889	12	
13	Moving expenses for members of the Armed Forces. Attach Form 3903	13	
14	Deductible part of self-employment tax. Attach Schedule SE	14	420.
15	Self-employed SEP, SIMPLE, and qualified plans	15	
16	Self-employed health insurance deduction	16	1,423.
17	Penalty on early withdrawal of savings	17	
18a	Alimony paid	18a	
b	Recipient's SSN . . . . ► _____		
c	Date of original divorce or separation agreement (see instructions) ► _____		
19	IRA deduction	19	
20	Student loan interest deduction	20	
21	Tuition and fees. Attach Form 8917	21	
22	Add lines 10 through 21. These are your **adjustments to income.** Enter here and on Form 1040 or 1040-SR, line 8a	22	1,843.

For Paperwork Reduction Act Notice, see your tax return instructions.   REV 09/08/20 Intuit.cg.cfp.sp   Schedule 1 (Form 1040 or 1040-SR) 2019

SCHEDULE 2
(Form 1040 or 1040-SR)

Department of the Treasury
Internal Revenue Service

Additional Taxes

▶ Attach to Form 1040 or 1040-SR.
▶ Go to *www.irs.gov/Form1040* for instructions and the latest information.

OMB No. 1545-0074

2019

Attachment
Sequence No. 02

Name(s) shown on Form 1040 or 1040-SR	Your social security number
Hussein M & Sharish K Abdulhusain	617-75-5679

Part I	**Tax**		
1	Alternative minimum tax. Attach Form 6251	1	
2	Excess advance premium tax credit repayment. Attach Form 8962	2	
3	Add lines 1 and 2. Enter here and include on Form 1040 or 1040-SR, line 12b	3	

Part II	**Other Taxes**		
4	Self-employment tax. Attach Schedule SE	4	840.
5	Unreported social security and Medicare tax from Form: a ☐ 4137 b ☐ 8919	5	
6	Additional tax on IRAs, other qualified retirement plans, and other tax-favored accounts. Attach Form 5329 if required	6	
7a	Household employment taxes. Attach Schedule H	7a	
b	Repayment of first-time homebuyer credit from Form 5405. Attach Form 5405 if required	7b	
8	Taxes from: a ☐ Form 8959 b ☐ Form 8960		
	c ☐ Instructions; enter code(s) _____	8	
9	Section 965 net tax liability installment from Form 965-A	9	
10	Add lines 4 through 8. These are your **total other taxes**. Enter here and on Form 1040 or 1040-SR, line 15	10	840.

For Paperwork Reduction Act Notice, see your tax return instructions.   REV 03/08/20 Intuit.cg.cfp.sp   Schedule 2 (Form 1040 or 1040-SR) 2019

SCHEDULE 3
(Form 1040 or 1040-SR)

Department of the Treasury
Internal Revenue Service

Additional Credits and Payments

▶ Attach to Form 1040 or 1040-SR.
▶ Go to *www.irs.gov/Form1040* for instructions and the latest information.

OMB No. 1545-0074

2019

Attachment
Sequence No. **03**

Name(s) shown on Form 1040 or 1040-SR

Hussein M & Sharish K Abdulhusain

Your social security number

617-75-5679

Part I	Nonrefundable Credits		
1	Foreign tax credit. Attach Form 1116 if required	1	
2	Credit for child and dependent care expenses. Attach Form 2441	2	
3	Education credits from Form 8863, line 19	3	
4	Retirement savings contributions credit. Attach Form 8880	4	
5	Residential energy credits. Attach Form 5695	5	
6	Other credits from Form: **a** ☐ 3800 **b** ☐ 8801 **c** ☐ _____	6	
7	Add lines 1 through 6. Enter here and include on Form 1040 or 1040-SR, line 13b	7	

Part II	Other Payments and Refundable Credits		
8	2019 estimated tax payments and amount applied from 2018 return	8	
9	Net premium tax credit. Attach Form 8962	9	1,596.
10	Amount paid with request for extension to file (see instructions)	10	
11	Excess social security and tier 1 RRTA tax withheld	11	
12	Credit for federal tax on fuels. Attach Form 4136	12	
13	Credits from Form: **a** ☐ 2439 **b** ☐ Reserved **c** ☐ 8885 **d** ☐ _____	13	
14	Add lines 8 through 13. Enter here and on Form 1040 or 1040-SR, line 18d	14	1,596.

For Paperwork Reduction Act Notice, see your tax return instructions.   REV 03/03/20 Intuit.cg.cfp.sp   Schedule 3 (Form 1040 or 1040-SR) 2019

SCHEDULE B
(Form 1040 or 1040-SR)

Department of the Treasury
Internal Revenue Service (99)

Interest and Ordinary Dividends

▶ Go to *www.irs.gov/ScheduleB* for instructions and the latest information.
▶ Attach to Form 1040 or 1040-SR.

OMB No. 1545-0074

2019

Attachment
Sequence No. 08

Name(s) shown on return

Hussein M & Sharish K Abdulhusain

Your social security number

617-75-5679

				Amount
Part I **Interest** (See instructions and the instructions for Forms 1040 and 1040-SR, line 2b.) **Note:** If you received a Form 1099-INT, Form 1099-OID, or substitute statement from a brokerage firm, list the firm's name as the payer and enter the total interest shown on that form.	1	List name of payer. If any interest is from a seller-financed mortgage and the buyer used the property as a personal residence, see the instructions and list this interest first. Also, show that buyer's social security number and address ▶	1	
	2	Add the amounts on line 1	2	
	3	Excludable interest on series EE and I U.S. savings bonds issued after 1989. Attach Form 8815	3	
	4	Subtract line 3 from line 2. Enter the result here and on Form 1040 or 1040-SR, line 2b . . . . ▶	4	

Note: If line 4 is over $1,500, you must complete Part III.

				Amount
Part II **Ordinary Dividends** (See instructions and the instructions for Forms 1040 and 1040-SR, line 3b.) **Note:** If you received a Form 1099-DIV or substitute statement from a brokerage firm, list the firm's name as the payer and enter the ordinary dividends shown on that form.	5	List name of payer ▶	5	
	6	Add the amounts on line 5. Enter the total here and on Form 1040 or 1040-SR, line 3b . . . . ▶	6	

Note: If line 6 is over $1,500, you must complete Part III.

Part III	You must complete this part if you **(a)** had over $1,500 of taxable interest or ordinary dividends; **(b)** had a foreign account; or **(c)** received a distribution from, or were a grantor of, or a transferor to, a foreign trust.		Yes	No
Foreign Accounts and Trusts **Caution:** If required, failure to file FinCEN Form 114 may result in substantial penalties. See instructions.	7a	At any time during 2019, did you have a financial interest in or signature authority over a financial account (such as a bank account, securities account, or brokerage account) located in a foreign country? See instructions	×	
		If "Yes," are you required to file FinCEN Form 114, Report of Foreign Bank and Financial Accounts (FBAR), to report that financial interest or signature authority? See FinCEN Form 114 and its instructions for filing requirements and exceptions to those requirements	×	
	b	If you are required to file FinCEN Form 114, enter the name of the foreign country where the financial account is located ▶ SA Saudi Arabia		
	8	During 2019, did you receive a distribution from, or were you the grantor of, or transferor to, a foreign trust? If "Yes," you may have to file Form 3520. See instructions		×

For Paperwork Reduction Act Notice, see your tax return instructions.   BAA   FDIA0401 11/14/19 xxx   Schedule B (Form 1040 or 1040-SR) 2019

SCHEDULE C
(Form 1040 or 1040-SR)

Department of the Treasury
Internal Revenue Service (99)

Profit or Loss From Business
(Sole Proprietorship)

▶ Go to www.irs.gov/ScheduleC for instructions and the latest information.
▶ Attach to Form 1040, 1040-SR, 1040-NR, or 1041; partnerships generally must file Form 1065.

OMB No. 1545-0074

2019

Attachment
Sequence No. 09

Name of proprietor	Social security number (SSN)
Hussein M Abdulhusain	617-75-5679

A	Principal business or profession, including product or service (see instructions)	B	Enter code from instructions
	Rideshare driving		▶ 4 8 5 3 0 0

C	Business name. If no separate business name, leave blank.	D	Employer ID number (EIN) (see instr.)
	Uber and Lyft		4 5 2 6 4 7 4 4 1

E   Business address (including suite or room no.) ▶ 2447 W Orange Ave
     City, town or post office, state, and ZIP code   Anaheim, CA 92804-3447

F   Accounting method: (1) ☒ Cash   (2) ☐ Accrual   (3) ☐ Other (specify) ▶ _____

G   Did you "materially participate" in the operation of this business during 2019? If "No," see instructions for limit on losses   ☒ Yes   ☐ No

H   If you started or acquired this business during 2019, check here   .   .   .   .   ▶ ☒

I   Did you make any payments in 2019 that would require you to file Form(s) 1099? (see instructions)   ☒ Yes   ☐ No

J   If "Yes," did you or will you file required Forms 1099?   .   .   .   .   ☒ Yes   ☐ No

Part I   Income

1	Gross receipts or sales. See instructions for line 1 and check the box if this income was reported to you on Form W-2 and the "Statutory employee" box on that form was checked . . . . . ▶ ☐	1	56,185.
2	Returns and allowances	2	
3	Subtract line 2 from line 1	3	56,185.
4	Cost of goods sold (from line 42)	4	
5	**Gross profit.** Subtract line 4 from line 3	5	56,185.
6	Other income, including federal and state gasoline or fuel tax credit or refund (see instructions) . .	6	
7	**Gross income.** Add lines 5 and 6 . . . . . ▶	7	56,185.

Part II   Expenses. Enter expenses for business use of your home **only** on line 30.

8	Advertising . . .	8		18	Office expense (see instructions)	18	
9	Car and truck expenses (see instructions). . .	9	34,958.	19	Pension and profit-sharing plans .	19	
				20	Rent or lease (see instructions):		
10	Commissions and fees	10		a	Vehicles, machinery, and equipment	20a	3,500.
11	Contract labor (see instructions)	11		b	Other business property . .	20b	
12	Depletion . . .	12		21	Repairs and maintenance . .	21	
13	Depreciation and section 179 expense deduction (not included in Part III) (see instructions) . . .	13		22	Supplies (not included in Part III)	22	510.
				23	Taxes and licenses . . .	23	
				24	Travel and meals:		
14	Employee benefit programs (other than on line 19) .	14		a	Travel	24a	
15	Insurance (other than health)	15		b	Deductible meals (see instructions) . . .	24b	
16	Interest (see instructions):			25	Utilities	25	495.
a	Mortgage (paid to banks, etc.)	16a		26	Wages (less employment credits) .	26	
b	Other . . .	16b		27a	Other expenses (from line 48) .	27a	10,778.
17	Legal and professional services	17		b	**Reserved for future use** . .	27b	
28	**Total expenses** before expenses for business use of home. Add lines 8 through 27a . . . ▶					28	50,241.
29	Tentative profit or (loss). Subtract line 28 from line 7					29	5,944.

30   Expenses for business use of your home. Do not report these expenses elsewhere. Attach Form 8829 unless using the simplified method (see instructions).

     Simplified method filers only: enter the total square footage of: (a) your home: _____

     and (b) the part of your home used for business: _____ . Use the Simplified Method Worksheet in the instructions to figure the amount to enter on line 30   .   .   .   . | 30 | |

31   **Net profit or (loss).** Subtract line 30 from line 29.

    • If a profit, enter on both **Schedule 1 (Form 1040 or 1040-SR), line 3** (or **Form 1040-NR, line 13**) and on **Schedule SE, line 2.** (If you checked the box on line 1, see instructions). Estates and trusts, enter on **Form 1041, line 3.**

    • If a loss, you **must** go to line 32. | 31 | 5,944. |

32   If you have a loss, check the box that describes your investment in this activity (see instructions).

    • If you checked 32a, enter the loss on both **Schedule 1 (Form 1040 or 1040-SR), line 3** (or **Form 1040-NR, line 13**) and on **Schedule SE, line 2.** (If you checked the box on line 1, see the line 31 instructions). Estates and trusts, enter on **Form 1041, line 3.**

    • If you checked 32b, you **must** attach Form 6198. Your loss may be limited.

32a ☐ All investment is at risk.
32b ☐ Some investment is not at risk.

For Paperwork Reduction Act Notice, see the separate instructions.   BAA   REV 12/06/20 Intuit.cg.cfp.sp   Schedule C (Form 1040 or 1040-SR) 2019

Part III   Cost of Goods Sold   (see instructions)

33   Method(s) used to
value closing inventory: a ☐ Cost   b ☐ Lower of cost or market   c ☐ Other (attach explanation)

34   Was there any change in determining quantities, costs, or valuations between opening and closing inventory?
If "Yes," attach explanation . . . . ☐ Yes   ☐ No

35   Inventory at beginning of year. If different from last year's closing inventory, attach explanation . . . | 35 |

36   Purchases less cost of items withdrawn for personal use . . . . | 36 |

37   Cost of labor. Do not include any amounts paid to yourself . . . . | 37 |

38   Materials and supplies . . . . | 38 |

39   Other costs . . . . | 39 |

40   Add lines 35 through 39 . . . . | 40 |

41   Inventory at end of year . . . . | 41 |

42   **Cost of goods sold.** Subtract line 41 from line 40. Enter the result here and on line 4 . . . . . . | 42 |

Part IV   Information on Your Vehicle. Complete this part **only** if you are claiming car or truck expenses on line 9 and are not required to file Form 4562 for this business. See the instructions for line 13 to find out if you must file Form 4562.

43   When did you place your vehicle in service for business purposes? (month, day, year)   ▶ 02/20/2019

44   Of the total number of miles you drove your vehicle during 2019, enter the number of miles you used your vehicle for:

a   Business   60,000   **b** Commuting (see instructions)   **c** Other   5,000

45   Was your vehicle available for personal use during off-duty hours? . . . . ☒ Yes   ☐ No

46   Do you (or your spouse) have another vehicle available for personal use? . . . . ☐ Yes   ☒ No

47a   Do you have evidence to support your deduction? . . . . ☒ Yes   ☐ No

b   If "Yes," is the evidence written? . . . . ☒ Yes   ☐ No

Part V   Other Expenses. List below business expenses not included on lines 8–26 or line 30.

Uber - Split Fare Fee	4.
Uber - Service Fee	4,738.
Uber - Booking Fee	6,036.

48   Total other expenses. Enter here and on line 27a . . . . | 48 | 10,778.

Self-Employment Tax

▶ Go to *www.irs.gov/ScheduleSE* for instructions and the latest information.
▶ Attach to Form 1040, 1040-SR, or 1040-NR.

OMB No. 1545-0074

2019

Attachment
Sequence No. **17**

Name of person with self-employment income (as shown on Form 1040, 1040-SR, or 1040-NR)	Social security number of person with self-employment income ▶
Hussein M Abdulhusain	617-75-5679

Before you begin: To determine if you must file Schedule SE, see the instructions.

May I Use Short Schedule SE or Must I Use Long Schedule SE?

Note: Use this flowchart **only if** you must file Schedule SE. If unsure, see *Who Must File Schedule SE* in the instructions.

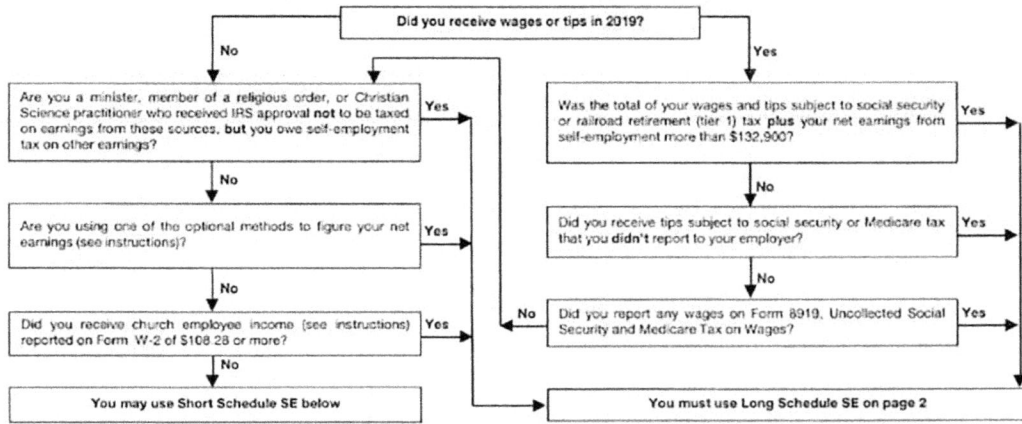

Did you receive wages or tips in 2019?

No

Are you a minister, member of a religious order, or Christian Science practitioner who received IRS approval **not** to be taxed on earnings from these sources, **but** you owe self-employment tax on other earnings? — Yes

No

Are you using one of the optional methods to figure your net earnings (see instructions)? — Yes

No

Did you receive church employee income (see instructions) reported on Form W-2 of $108.28 or more? — Yes

No

You may use Short Schedule SE below

Yes

Was the total of your wages and tips subject to social security or railroad retirement (tier 1) tax **plus** your net earnings from self-employment more than $132,900? — Yes

No

Did you receive tips subject to social security or Medicare tax that you didn't report to your employer? — Yes

No

No — Did you report any wages on Form 8919, Uncollected Social Security and Medicare Tax on Wages? — Yes

You must use Long Schedule SE on page 2

Section A—Short Schedule SE. Caution: Read above to see if you can use Short Schedule SE.

1a	Net farm profit or (loss) from Schedule F, line 34, and farm partnerships, Schedule K-1 (Form 1065), box 14, code A	**1a**	
b	If you received social security retirement or disability benefits, enter the amount of Conservation Reserve Program payments included on Schedule F, line 4b, or listed on Schedule K-1 (Form 1065), box 20, code AH	**1b**	( )
2	Net profit or (loss) from Schedule C, line 31; and Schedule K-1 (Form 1065), box 14, code A (other than farming). Ministers and members of religious orders, see instructions for types of income to report on this line. See instructions for other income to report	**2**	5,944.
3	Combine lines 1a, 1b, and 2	**3**	5,944.
4	Multiply line 3 by 92.35% (0.9235). If less than $400, you don't owe self-employment tax; **don't file** this schedule unless you have an amount on line 1b ▶	**4**	5,489.
	Note: If line 4 is less than $400 due to Conservation Reserve Program payments on line 1b, see instructions.		
5	**Self-employment tax.** If the amount on line 4 is: • $132,900 or less, multiply line 4 by 15.3% (0.153). Enter the result here and on **Schedule 2 (Form 1040 or 1040-SR), line 4,** or **Form 1040-NR, line 55.** • More than $132,900, multiply line 4 by 2.9% (0.029). Then, add $16,479.60 to the result. Enter the total here and on **Schedule 2 (Form 1040 or 1040-SR), line 4,** or **Form 1040-NR, line 55** .	**5**	840.
6	**Deduction for one-half of self-employment tax.** Multiply line 5 by 50% (0.50). Enter the result here and on **Schedule 1 (Form 1040 or 1040-SR), line 14,** or **Form 1040-NR, line 27**	**6**	420.

For Paperwork Reduction Act Notice, see your tax return instructions.   BAA   REV 03/08/20 ntuitepicb in   Schedule SE (Form 1040 or 1040-SR) 2019

SCHEDULE EIC
(Form 1040 or 1040-SR)

Department of the Treasury
Internal Revenue Service (99)

Earned Income Credit

Qualifying Child Information

▶ Complete and attach to Form 1040 or 1040-SR only if you have a qualifying child.
▶ Go to *www.irs.gov/ScheduleEIC* for the latest information.

OMB No. 1545-0074

2019

Attachment
Sequence No. **43**

Name(s) shown on return
Hussein M & Sharish K Abdulhusain

Your social security number
617-75-5679

Before you begin:
- See the instructions for Form 1040 or 1040-SR, line 18a, to make sure that (a) you can take the EIC, and (b) you have a qualifying child.
- Be sure the child's name on line 1 and social security number (SSN) on line 2 agree with the child's social security card. Otherwise, at the time we process your return, we may reduce or disallow your EIC. If the name or SSN on the child's social security card is not correct, call the Social Security Administration at 1-800-772-1213.

- *You can't claim the EIC for a child who didn't live with you for more than half of the year.*
- *If you take the EIC even though you are not eligible, you may not be allowed to take the credit for up to 10 years. See the instructions for details.*
- *It will take us longer to process your return and issue your refund if you do not fill in all lines that apply for each qualifying child.*

Qualifying Child Information	Child 1		Child 2		Child 3	
1 Child's name If you have more than three qualifying children, you have to list only three to get the maximum credit.	First name	Last name	First name	Last name	First name	Last name
	Ayaan H Abdulhusain					
2 Child's SSN The child must have an SSN as defined in the instructions for Form 1040 or 1040-SR, line 18a, unless the child was born and died in 2019. If your child was born and died in 2019 and did not have an SSN, enter "Died" on this line and attach a copy of the child's birth certificate, death certificate, or hospital medical records showing a live birth.	891-56-7642					
3 Child's year of birth	Year 2 0 1 9		Year _ _ _ _		Year _ _ _ _	
4 a Was the child under age 24 at the end of 2019, a student, and younger than you (or your spouse, if filing jointly)?	☐ Yes.	☐ No.	☐ Yes.	☐ No.	☐ Yes.	☐ No.
b Was the child permanently and totally disabled during any part of 2019?	☐ Yes.	☐ No. The child is not a qualifying child.	☐ Yes.	☐ No. The child is not a qualifying child.	☐ Yes.	☐ No. The child is not a qualifying child.
5 Child's relationship to you (for example, son, daughter, grandchild, niece, nephew, eligible foster child, etc.)	Son					
6 Number of months child lived with you in the United States during 2019 • If the child lived with you for more than half of 2019 but less than 7 months, enter "7." • If the child was born or died in 2019 and your home was the child's home for more than half the time he or she was alive during 2019, enter "12."	12 months *Do not enter more than 12 months.*		____ months *Do not enter more than 12 months.*		____ months *Do not enter more than 12 months.*	

For Paperwork Reduction Act Notice, see your tax return instructions.

BAA

REV 03/08/20 Intuit.cg.cfp.sp

Schedule EIC (Form 1040 or 1040-SR) 2019

Additional Child Tax Credit

▶ Attach to Form 1040, 1040-SR, or 1040-NR.
▶ Go to *www.irs.gov/Schedule8812* for instructions and the latest information.

OMB No. 1545-0074

2019

Attachment
Sequence No. **47**

Name(s) shown on return	Your social security number
Hussein M & Sharish K Abdulhusain	617-75-5679

Part I   All Filers

Caution: If you file Form 2555, **stop here;** you cannot claim the additional child tax credit.

1	If you are required to use the worksheet in Pub. 972, enter the amount from line 10 of the Child Tax Credit and Credit for Other Dependents Worksheet in the publication. Otherwise:		
	1040 and 1040-SR filers: Enter the amount from line 8 of your Child Tax Credit and Credit for Other Dependents Worksheet (see the instructions for Forms 1040 and 1040-SR, line 13a).		
	1040-NR filers: Enter the amount from line 8 of your Child Tax Credit and Credit for Other Dependents Worksheet (see the instructions for Form 1040-NR, line 49).	**1**	2,000.
2	Enter the amount from Form 1040, line 13a; Form 1040-SR, line 13a; or Form 1040-NR, line 49	**2**	0.
3	Subtract line 2 from line 1. If zero, **stop here;** you cannot claim this credit	**3**	2,000.
4	Number of qualifying children under 17 with the required social security number: _____1_____ x $1,400. Enter the result. If zero, **stop here;** you cannot claim this credit	**4**	1,400.
	TIP: The number of children you use for this line is the same as the number of children you used for line 1 of the Child Tax Credit and Credit for Other Dependents Worksheet.		
5	Enter the **smaller** of line 3 or line 4	**5**	1,400.
6a	Earned income (see instructions)	**6a**	7,625.
b	Nontaxable combat pay (see instructions) **6b**		
7	Is the amount on line 6a more than $2,500?		
	☐ **No.** Leave line 7 blank and enter -0- on line 8.		
	☒ **Yes.** Subtract $2,500 from the amount on line 6a. Enter the result	**7**	5,125.
8	Multiply the amount on line 7 by 15% (0.15) and enter the result	**8**	769.
	Next. On line 4, is the amount $4,200 or more?		
	☒ **No.** If line 8 is zero, **stop here;** you cannot claim this credit. Otherwise, skip Part II and enter the **smaller** of line 5 or line 8 on line 15.		
	☐ **Yes.** If line 8 is equal to or more than line 5, skip Part II and enter the amount from line 5 on line 15. Otherwise, go to line 9.		

Part II   Certain Filers Who Have Three or More Qualifying Children

9	Withheld social security, Medicare, and Additional Medicare taxes from Form(s) W-2, boxes 4 and 6. If married filing jointly, include your spouse's amounts with yours. If your employer withheld or you paid Additional Medicare Tax or tier 1 RRTA taxes, see instructions	**9**	
10	**1040 and 1040-SR filers:** Enter the total of the amounts from Schedule 1 (Form 1040 or 1040-SR), line 14, and Schedule 2 (Form 1040 or 1040-SR), line 5, plus any taxes that you identified using code "UT" and entered on Schedule 2 (Form 1040 or 1040-SR), line 8.		
	1040-NR filers: Enter the total of the amounts from Form 1040-NR, lines 27 and 56, plus any taxes that you identified using code "UT" and entered on line 60.	**10**	
11	Add lines 9 and 10	**11**	
12	**1040 and 1040-SR filers:** Enter the total of the amounts from Form 1040 or 1040-SR, line 18a, and Schedule 3 (Form 1040 or 1040-SR), line 11.		
	1040-NR filers: Enter the amount from Form 1040-NR, line 67.	**12**	
13	Subtract line 12 from line 11. If zero or less, enter -0-	**13**	
14	Enter the **larger** of line 8 or line 13	**14**	
	Next, enter the **smaller** of line 5 or line 14 on line 15.		

Part III   Additional Child Tax Credit

15	This is your additional child tax credit	**15**	769.

Enter this amount on
Form 1040, line 18b;
Form 1040-SR, line 18b; or
Form 1040-NR, line 64.

Form **8995**

Department of the Treasury
Internal Revenue Service

Qualified Business Income Deduction
Simplified Computation

▶ Attach to your tax return.
▶ Go to *www.irs.gov/Form8995* for instructions and the latest information.

OMB No. 1545-0123

2019

Attachment
Sequence No. **55**

Name(s) shown on return
Hussein M & Sharish K Abdulhusain

Your taxpayer identification number
617-75-5679

1	(a) Trade, business, or aggregation name	(b) Taxpayer identification number	(c) Qualified business income or (loss)
i	Uber and Lyft	452647441	4,101.
ii			
iii			
iv			
v			

2	Total qualified business income or (loss). Combine lines 1i through 1v, column (c)	2	4,101.	
3	Qualified business net (loss) carryforward from the prior year	3	( )	
4	Total qualified business income. Combine lines 2 and 3. If zero or less, enter -0-	4	4,101.	
5	Qualified business income component. Multiply line 4 by 20% (0.20)			5	820.
6	Qualified REIT dividends and publicly traded partnership (PTP) income or (loss) (see instructions)	6		
7	Qualified REIT dividends and qualified PTP (loss) carryforward from the prior year	7	( )	
8	Total qualified REIT dividends and PTP income. Combine lines 6 and 7. If zero or less, enter -0-	8		
9	REIT and PTP component. Multiply line 8 by 20% (0.20)			9	
10	Qualified business income deduction before the income limitation. Add lines 5 and 9			10	820.
11	Taxable income before qualified business income deduction	11	0.	
12	Net capital gain (see instructions)	12	0.	
13	Subtract line 12 from line 11. If zero or less, enter -0-	13	0.	
14	Income limitation. Multiply line 13 by 20% (0.20)			14	0.
15	Qualified business income deduction. Enter the lesser of line 10 or line 14. Also enter this amount on the applicable line of your return ▶			15	0.
16	Total qualified business (loss) carryforward. Combine lines 2 and 3. If greater than zero, enter -0-			16	(0.)
17	Total qualified REIT dividends and PTP (loss) carryforward. Combine lines 6 and 7. If greater than zero, enter -0-			17	(0.)

For Privacy Act and Paperwork Reduction Act Notice, see instructions.

Form **8995** (2019)

Form **8962**	**Premium Tax Credit (PTC)**	OMB No. 1545-0074

Department of the Treasury
Internal Revenue Service

► Attach to Form 1040, 1040-SR, or 1040-NR.
► Go to *www.irs.gov/Form8962* for instructions and the latest information.

2019
Attachment
Sequence No. **73**

Name shown on your return: Hussein M & Sharish K Abdulhusain

Your social security number: 617-75-5679

You cannot take the PTC if your filing status is married filing separately unless you qualify for an exception (see instructions). If you qualify, check the box . . . ► ☐

Part I   Annual and Monthly Contribution Amount

1	Tax family size. Enter your tax family size (see instructions)	**1**	3
2a	Modified AGI. Enter your modified AGI (see instructions) . . . . **2a** 6,202.		
b	Enter the total of your dependents' modified AGI (see instructions) **2b**		
3	Household income. Add the amounts on lines 2a and 2b (see instructions)	**3**	6,202.
4	Federal poverty line. Enter the federal poverty line amount from Table 1-1, 1-2, or 1-3 (see instructions). Check the appropriate box for the federal poverty table used. a ☐ Alaska b ☐ Hawaii c ☒ Other 48 states and DC	**4**	20,780.
5	Household income as a percentage of federal poverty line (see instructions)	**5**	29 %
6	Did you enter 401% on line 5? (See instructions if you entered less than 100%.)		
	☒ **No.** Continue to line 7.		
	☐ **Yes.** You are not eligible to take the PTC. If advance payment of the PTC was made, see the instructions for how to report your excess advance PTC repayment amount.		
7	Applicable Figure. Using your line 5 percentage, locate your "applicable figure" on the table in the instructions . .	**7**	0.0208
8a	Annual contribution amount. Multiply line 3 by line 7. Round to nearest whole dollar amount **8a** 129.	b Monthly contribution amount. Divide line 8a by 12. Round to nearest whole dollar amount	**8b**	11.

Part II   Premium Tax Credit Claim and Reconciliation of Advance Payment of Premium Tax Credit

9	Are you allocating policy amounts with another taxpayer or do you want to use the alternative calculation for year of marriage (see instructions)?
	☐ **Yes.** Skip to Part IV, Allocation of Policy Amounts, or Part V, Alternative Calculation for Year of Marriage. ☒ **No.** Continue to line 10.
10	See the instructions to determine if you can use line 11 or must complete lines 12 through 23.
	☒ **Yes.** Continue to line 11. Compute your annual PTC. Then skip lines 12–23 and continue to line 24. ☐ **No.** Continue to lines 12–23. Compute your monthly PTC and continue to line 24.

Annual Calculation	(a) Annual enrollment premiums (Form(s) 1095-A, line 33A)	(b) Annual applicable SLCSP premium (Form(s) 1095-A, line 33B)	(c) Annual contribution amount (line 8a)	(d) Annual maximum premium assistance (subtract (c) from (b), if zero or less, enter -0-)	(e) Annual premium tax credit allowed (smaller of (a) or (d))	(f) Annual advance payment of PTC (Form(s) 1095-A, line 33C)
11 Annual Totals	10,452.	9,029.	129.	8,900.	8,900.	7,304.

Monthly Calculation	(a) Monthly enrollment premiums (Form(s) 1095-A, lines 21–32, column A)	(b) Monthly applicable SLCSP premium (Form(s) 1095-A, lines 21–32, column B)	(c) Monthly contribution amount (amount from line 8b or alternative marriage monthly calculation)	(d) Monthly maximum premium assistance (subtract (c) from (b), if zero or less, enter -0-)	(e) Monthly premium tax credit allowed (smaller of (a) or (d))	(f) Monthly advance payment of PTC (Form(s) 1095-A, lines 21–32, column C)
12 January						
13 February						
14 March						
15 April						
16 May						
17 June						
18 July						
19 August						
20 September						
21 October						
22 November						
23 December						

24	Total premium tax credit. Enter the amount from line 11(e) or add lines 12(e) through 23(e) and enter the total here	**24**	8,900.
25	Advance payment of PTC. Enter the amount from line 11(f) or add lines 12(f) through 23(f) and enter the total here	**25**	7,304.
26	Net premium tax credit. If line 24 is greater than line 25, subtract line 25 from line 24. Enter the difference here and on Schedule 3 (Form 1040 or 1040-SR), line 9, or Form 1040-NR, line 65. If line 24 equals line 25, enter -0-. Stop here. If line 25 is greater than line 24, leave this line blank and continue to line 27	**26**	1,596.

Part III   Repayment of Excess Advance Payment of the Premium Tax Credit

27	Excess advance payment of PTC. If line 25 is greater than line 24, subtract line 24 from line 25. Enter the difference here	**27**	
28	Repayment limitation (see instructions)	**28**	
29	Excess advance premium tax credit repayment. Enter the smaller of line 27 or line 28 here and on Schedule 2 (Form 1040 or 1040-SR), line 2, or Form 1040-NR, line 44	**29**	

For Paperwork Reduction Act Notice, see your tax return instructions.   BA   REV 03/08/20 Intuit   Form **8962** (2019)

Part IV — Allocation of Policy Amounts

Complete the following information for up to four policy amount allocations. See instructions for allocation details.

Allocation 1

30	(a) Policy Number (Form 1095-A, line 2)	(b) SSN of other taxpayer	(c) Allocation start month	(d) Allocation stop month

Allocation percentage applied to monthly amounts	(e) Premium Percentage	(f) SLCSP Percentage	(g) Advance Payment of the PTC Percentage

Allocation 2

31	(a) Policy Number (Form 1095-A, line 2)	(b) SSN of other taxpayer	(c) Allocation start month	(d) Allocation stop month

Allocation percentage applied to monthly amounts	(e) Premium Percentage	(f) SLCSP Percentage	(g) Advance Payment of the PTC Percentage

Allocation 3

32	(a) Policy Number (Form 1095-A, line 2)	(b) SSN of other taxpayer	(c) Allocation start month	(d) Allocation stop month

Allocation percentage applied to monthly amounts	(e) Premium Percentage	(f) SLCSP Percentage	(g) Advance Payment of the PTC Percentage

Allocation 4

33	(a) Policy Number (Form 1095-A, line 2)	(b) SSN of other taxpayer	(c) Allocation start month	(d) Allocation stop month

Allocation percentage applied to monthly amounts	(e) Premium Percentage	(f) SLCSP Percentage	(g) Advance Payment of the PTC Percentage

34   Have you completed all policy amount allocations?

☐ **Yes.** Multiply the amounts on Form 1095-A by the allocation percentages entered by policy. Add all allocated policy amounts and non-allocated policy amounts from Forms 1095-A, if any, to compute a combined total for each month. Enter the combined total for each month on lines 12–23, columns (a), (b), and (f). Compute the amounts for lines 12–23, columns (c)–(e), and continue to line 24.

☐ **No.** See the instructions to report additional policy amount allocations.

Part V — Alternative Calculation for Year of Marriage

Complete line(s) 35 and/or 36 to elect the alternative calculation for year of marriage. For eligibility to make the election, see the instructions for line 9. To complete line(s) 35 and/or 36 and compute the amounts for lines 12–23, see the instructions for this Part V.

		(a) Alternative family size	(b) Alternative monthly contribution amount	(c) Alternative start month	(d) Alternative stop month
35	Alternative entries for your SSN				
36	Alternative entries for your spouse's SSN				

2019 California Resident Income Tax Return

FORM **540**

APE   ATTACH FEDERAL RETURN

617-75-5679 ABDU 730-18-6921
HUSSEIN M ABDULHUSAIN
SHARISH K ABDULHUSAIN

2447 W ORANGE AVE
ANAHEIM   CA 92804-3447

08-10-1989 10-24-1987

19   PBA   485300

Filing Status

If your California filing status is different from your federal filing status, check the box here . . . . ☐

1 ☐ Single

2 ☒ Married/RDP filing jointly. See inst.

3 ☐ Married/RDP filing separately. Enter spouse's/RDP's SSN or ITIN above and full name here

4 ☐ Head of household (with qualifying person). See instructions.

5 ☐ Qualifying widow(er). Enter year spouse/RDP died. ☐
See instructions.

6 If someone can claim you (or your spouse/RDP) as a dependent, check the box here. See inst . . . . ● 6 ☐

Exemptions

► For line 7, line 8, line 9, and line 10: Multiply the number you enter in the box by the pre-printed dollar amount for that line.   **Whole dollars only**

7 **Personal:** If you checked box 1, 3, or 4 above, enter 1 in the box. If you checked box 2 or 5, enter 2 in the box. If you checked the box on line 6, see instructions. ● 7 | 2 | X $122 = ● $ | 244 |

8 **Blind:** If you (or your spouse/RDP) are visually impaired, enter 1; if both are visually impaired, enter 2. . . . . ● 8 | | X $122 = ● $ | |

9 **Senior:** If you (or your spouse/RDP) are 65 or older, enter 1; if both are 65 or older, enter 2 . . . . ● 9 | | X $122 = ● $ | |

10 **Dependents:** Do not include yourself or your spouse/RDP.

	Dependent 1	Dependent 2	Dependent 3
First Name	● AYAAN H	●	●
Last Name	● ABDULHUSAIN	●	●
SSN	● 891567642	●	●
Dependent's relationship to you	● SON	●	●

Total dependent exemptions . . . . ● 10 | 1 | X $378 = ● $ | 378 |

REV 09/09/20 INTUIT CG CFP SP

175   3101194   Form 540 2019 **Side 1**

Your name: ABDULHUSAIN   Your SSN or ITIN: 617-75-5679

11 Exemption amount: Add line 7 through line 10. Transfer this amount to line 32 . . . .   ● **11** $ [622]

Taxable Income

12 State wages from your federal Form(s) W-2,
box 16 . . . .   ● **12** [2101] .00

13 Enter federal adjusted gross income from federal Form 1040 or 1040-SR, line 8b . . . . . .   ● **13** [6202] .00
14 California adjustments – subtractions. Enter the amount from Schedule CA (540),
Part I, line 23, column B . . . .   ● **14** [   ] .00
15 Subtract line 14 from line 13. If less than zero, enter the result in parentheses.
See instructions . . . .   **15** [6202] .00
16 California adjustments – additions. Enter the amount from Schedule CA (540),
Part I, line 23, column C . . . .   ● **16** [   ] .00
17 California adjusted gross income. Combine line 15 and line 16 . . . .   ● **17** [6202] .00
18 Enter the larger of
| Your California **itemized deductions** from Schedule CA (540), Part II, line 30; **OR**
| Your California **standard deduction** shown below for your filing status:
  • Single or Married/RDP filing separately $4,537
  • Married/RDP filing jointly, Head of household, or Qualifying widow(er) $9,074
If Married/RDP filing separately or the box on line 6 is checked, STOP. See instructions   ● **18** [10265] .00
19 Subtract line 18 from line 17. This is your **taxable income**.
If less than zero, enter -0- . . . .   ● **19** [0] .00

Tax

31 Tax. Check the box if from   [X] Tax Table   [ ] Tax Rate Schedule
● [ ] FTB 3800   ● [ ] FTB 3803 . . . .   ● **31** [0] .00
32 Exemption credits. Enter the amount from line 11. If your federal AGI is more than $200,534,
see instructions . . . .   ● **32** [622] .00
33 Subtract line 32 from line 31. If less than zero, enter -0- . . . .   ● **33** [0] .00
34 Tax. See instructions. Check the box if from: ● [ ] Schedule G-1 ● [ ] FTB 5870A   ● **34** [   ] .00
35 Add line 33 and line 34 . . . .   ● **35** [0] .00

Special Credits

40 Nonrefundable Child and Dependent Care Expenses Credit. See instructions . . . .   ● **40** [   ] .00
43 Enter credit name [   ] code ● [   ] and amount . . .   ● **43** [   ] .00
44 Enter credit name [   ] code ● [   ] and amount . . .   ● **44** [   ] .00
45 To claim more than two credits. See instructions. Attach Schedule P (540) . . . .   ● **45** [   ] .00
46 Nonrefundable renter's credit. See instructions . . . .   ● **46** [   ] .00
47 Add line 40 through line 46. These are your total credits . . . .   ● **47** [   ] .00
48 Subtract line 47 from line 35. If less than zero, enter -0- . . . .   ● **48** [0] .00

Your name: ABDULHUSAIN   Your SSN or ITIN: 617-75-5679

Other Taxes

61	Alternative minimum tax. Attach Schedule P (540)	● 61	.00
62	Mental Health Services Tax. See instructions	● 62	.00
63	Other taxes and credit recapture. See instructions	● 63	.00
64	Add line 48, line 61, line 62, and line 63. This is your total tax	● 64	0 .00

Payments

71	California income tax withheld. See instructions	● 71	16 .00
72	2019 CA estimated tax and other payments. See instructions	● 72	.00
73	Withholding (Form 592-B and/or 593). See instructions	● 73	.00
74	Excess SDI (or VPDI) withheld. See instructions	● 74	.00
75	Earned Income Tax Credit (EITC)	● 75	1012 .00
76	Young Child Tax Credit (YCTC). See instructions	● 76	1000 .00
77	Add lines 71 through 76. These are your total payments. See instructions	◉ 77	2028 .00

Use Tax

91	Use Tax. Do not leave blank. See instructions	● 91	0 .00

If line 91 is zero, check if: [X] No use tax is owed.

[ ] You paid your use tax obligation directly to CDTFA.

Overpaid Tax/Tax Due

92	Payments balance. If line 77 is more than line 91, subtract line 91 from line 77	◉ 92	2028 .00
93	**Use Tax balance.** If line 91 is more than line 77, subtract line 77 from line 91	◉ 93	.00
94	Overpaid tax. If line 92 is more than line 64, subtract line 64 from line 92	◉ 94	2028 .00
95	Amount of line 94 you want applied to your **2020** estimated tax	● 95	.00
96	Overpaid tax available this year. Subtract line 95 from line 94	● 96	2028 .00
97	Tax due. If line 92 is less than line 64, subtract line 92 from line 64	◉ 97	.00

Your name: ABDULHUSAIN Your SSN or ITIN: 617-75-5679

	Code	Amount
California Seniors Special Fund. See instructions	● 400	.00
Alzheimer's Disease and Related Dementia Voluntary Tax Contribution Fund	● 401	.00
Rare and Endangered Species Preservation Voluntary Tax Contribution Program	● 403	.00
California Breast Cancer Research Voluntary Tax Contribution Fund	● 405	.00
California Firefighters' Memorial Fund	● 406	.00
Emergency Food for Families Voluntary Tax Contribution Fund	● 407	.00
California Peace Officer Memorial Foundation Fund	● 408	.00
California Sea Otter Fund	● 410	.00
California Cancer Research Voluntary Tax Contribution Fund	● 413	.00
School Supplies for Homeless Children Fund	● 422	.00
State Parks Protection Fund/Parks Pass Purchase	● 423	.00
Protect Our Coast and Oceans Voluntary Tax Contribution Fund	● 424	.00
Keep Arts in Schools Voluntary Tax Contribution Fund	● 425	.00
Prevention of Animal Homelessness and Cruelty Voluntary Tax Contribution Fund	● 431	.00
California Senior Citizen Advocacy Voluntary Tax Contribution Fund	● 438	.00
Native California Wildlife Rehabilitation Voluntary Tax Contribution Fund	● 439	.00
Rape Kit Backlog Voluntary Tax Contribution Fund	● 440	.00
Organ and Tissue Donor Registry Voluntary Tax Contribution Fund	● 441	.00
National Alliance on Mental Illness California Voluntary Tax Contribution Fund	● 442	.00
Schools Not Prisons Voluntary Tax Contribution Fund	● 443	.00
Suicide Prevention Voluntary Tax Contribution Fund	● 444	.00
110 Add code 400 through code 444. This is your total contribution	● 110	.00

Contributions

Your name: ABDULHUSAIN Your SSN or ITIN: 617-75-5679

Amount You Owe

111 AMOUNT YOU OWE. If you do not have an amount on line 96, add line 93, line 97, and line 110. See instructions. **Do not send cash.**
Mail to: FRANCHISE TAX BOARD, PO BOX 942867, SACRAMENTO CA 94267-0001 ..... ● 111 [ ] .00
Pay Online – Go to ftb.ca.gov/pay for more information.

Interest and Penalties

112 Interest, late return penalties, and late payment penalties .... 112 [ ] .00

113 Underpayment of estimated tax.
Check the box: ● [ ] FTB 5805 attached ● [ ] FTB 5805F attached .... ● 113 [ ] .00

114 Total amount due. See instructions. Enclose, but **do not staple**, any payment .... 114 [ ] .00

115 **REFUND OR NO AMOUNT DUE.** Subtract the sum of 110, line 112 and line 113 from line 96. See instructions.

Mail to: FRANCHISE TAX BOARD, PO BOX 942840, SACRAMENTO CA 94240-0001 ...... ● 115 [2028] .00

Refund and Direct Deposit

Fill in the information to authorize direct deposit of your refund into one or two accounts. **Do not** attach a voided check or a deposit slip.
See instructions. **Have you verified the routing and account numbers?** Use whole dollars only.

All or the following amount of my refund (line 115) is authorized for direct deposit into the account shown below:

● Routing number ● Type [X] Checking ● Account number ● 116 Direct deposit amount
[121000358] [ ] Savings [002345668506] [2028] .00

The remaining amount of my refund (line 115) is authorized for direct deposit into the account shown below:

● Routing number ● Type [ ] Checking ● Account number ● 117 Direct deposit amount
[ ] [ ] Savings [ ] [ ] .00

IMPORTANT: See the instructions to find out if you should attach a copy of your complete federal tax return.

To learn about your privacy rights, how we may use your information, and the consequences for not providing the requested information, go to **ftb.ca.gov/forms** and search for **1131**. To request this notice by mail, call 800.852.5711.

Under penalties of perjury, I declare that I have examined this tax return, including accompanying schedules and statements, and to the best of my knowledge and belief, it is true, correct, and complete.

Your signature [ ] Date [ ] Spouse's/RDP's signature (if a joint tax return, both must sign) [ ]

Sign Here

It is unlawful to forge a spouse's/RDP's signature

Joint tax return? (See instructions)

● Your email address. Enter only one email address. [ ] ● Preferred phone number [3109994788]

Paid preparer's signature (declaration of preparer is based on all information of which preparer has any knowledge)
[SELF-PREPARED]

Firm's name (or yours, if self-employed) [ ] ● PTIN [ ]

Firm's address [ ] ● Firm's FEIN [ ]

Do you want to allow another person to discuss this tax return with us? See instructions .... ● [ ] Yes [X] No

Print Third Party Designee's Name [ ] Telephone Number [ ]

REV 03/06/20 NSJF C8 CPP SP   175   3105194   Form 540 2019 Side 5

2019 California Adjustments — Residents

SCHEDULE

CA (540)

Important: Attach this schedule behind Form 540, Side 5 as a supporting California schedule.

Name(s) as shown on tax return

HUSSEIN M & SHARISH K ABDULHUSAIN

SSN or ITIN

617755679

Part I Income Adjustment Schedule

Section A – Income from federal Form 1040 or 1040-SR

			A Federal Amounts (taxable amounts from your federal tax return)	B Subtractions See instructions	C Additions See instructions
1	Wages, salaries, tips, etc. See instructions before making an entry in column B or C	1	2,101.		
2	Taxable interest. a	2b			
3	Ordinary dividends. See instructions. a	3b			
4	IRA distributions. See instructions. a	4b			
	c Pensions and annuities. See instructions. c	4d			
5	Social security benefits. a	5b			
6	Capital gain or (loss). See instructions	6			

Section B – Additional Income from federal Schedule 1 (Form 1040 or 1040-SR)

1	Taxable refunds, credits, or offsets of state and local income taxes	1			
2a	Alimony received	2a			
3	Business income or (loss)	3	5,944.		
4	Other gains or (losses)	4			
5	Rental real estate, royalties, partnerships, S corporations, trusts, etc	5			
6	Farm income or (loss)	6			
7	Unemployment compensation	7			
8	Other income.	8		a b c d e f g	a b c d e f g

a California lottery winnings
b Disaster loss deduction from FTB 3805V
c Federal NOL (federal Schedule 1 (Form 1040 or 1040-SR), line 8)
d NOL deduction from FTB 3805V
e NOL from FTB 3805Z, 3806, 3807, or 3809
f Other (describe):
g Student loan discharged due to closure of a for-profit school

9	**Total.** Combine Section A, line 1 through line 6, and Section B, line 1 through line 8 in column A. Add Section A, line 1 through line 6, and Section B, line 1 through line 8g in column B and column C. Go to Section C	9	8,045.		

Section C – Adjustments to Income from federal Schedule 1 (Form 1040 or 1040-SR)

10	Educator expenses	10			
11	Certain business expenses of reservists, performing artists, and fee-basis government officials	11			
12	Health savings account deduction	12			
13	Moving expenses. Attach federal Form 3903. See instructions	13			
14	Deductible part of self-employment tax	14	420.		
15	Self-employed SEP, SIMPLE, and qualified plans	15			
16	Self-employed health insurance deduction	16	1,423.		
17	Penalty on early withdrawal of savings	17			
18a	Alimony paid. b Recipient's: SSN ___ ___ – ___ ___ – ___ ___ ___ Last name	18a			
19	IRA deduction	19			
20	Student loan interest deduction	20			
21	Tuition and fees	21			
22	Add line 10 through line 18a and line 19 through line 21 in columns A, B, and C. See instructions	22	1,843.		
23	**Total.** Subtract line 22 from line 9 in columns A, B, and C. See instructions	23	6,202.		

Part II Adjustments to Federal Itemized Deductions

Check the box if you did NOT itemize for federal but will itemize for California . . . . ⊙ ☒

			A Federal Amounts (from federal Schedule A (Form 1040 or 1040-SR))	B Subtractions See instructions	C Additions See instructions
Medical and Dental Expenses See instructions.					
1	Medical and dental expenses . . . . ⊙ 10,530.	1			
2	Enter amount from federal Form 1040 or 1040-SR, line 8b ⊙ 6,202.	2			
3	Multiply line 2 by 7.5% (0.075) . . . . ⊙ 465.	3			
4	Subtract line 3 from line 1. If line 3 is more than line 1, enter 0.	4	⊙ 10,065.		⊙ 0.
Taxes You Paid					
5a	State and local income tax or general sales taxes.	5a	⊙ 37.	⊙ 37.	
5b	State and local real estate taxes	5b	⊙		
5c	State and local personal property taxes	5c	⊙ 200.		
5d	Add lines 5a through 5c	5d	⊙ 237.		
5e	Enter the smaller of line 5d or $10,000 ($5,000 if married filing separately) in column A . . .				
	Enter the amount from line 5a, column B in line 5e, column B				
	Enter the difference from line 5d and line 5e, column A in line 5e, column C	5e	⊙ 237.	⊙ 37.	⊙ 0.
6	Other taxes. List type ⊙ _____	6	⊙	⊙	⊙
7	Add lines 5e and 6	7	⊙ 237.	⊙ 37.	⊙ 0.
Interest You Paid					
8a	Home mortgage interest and points reported to you on Form 1098.	8a	⊙		⊙
8b	Home mortgage interest not reported to you on Form 1098	8b	⊙		⊙
8c	Points not reported to you on Form 1098.	8c	⊙		⊙
8d	Mortgage insurance premiums	8d	⊙	⊙	
8e	Add lines 8a through 8d	8e	⊙	⊙	⊙
9	Investment interest.	9	⊙	⊙	⊙
10	Add lines 8e and 9	10	⊙	⊙	⊙
Gifts to Charity					
11	Gifts by cash or check	11	⊙	⊙	⊙
12	Other than by cash or check.	12	⊙	⊙	⊙
13	Carryover from prior year.	13	⊙	⊙	⊙
14	Add lines 11 through 13.	14	⊙	⊙	⊙
Casualty and Theft Losses					
15	Casualty or theft loss(es) (other than net qualified disaster losses). Attach federal Form 4684. See instructions.	15	⊙	⊙	⊙
Other Itemized Deductions					
16	Other—from list in federal instructions	16	⊙	⊙	⊙
17	Add lines 4, 7, 10, 14, 15, and 16 in columns A, B, and C	17	⊙ 10,302.	⊙ 37.	⊙ 0.
18	Total. Combine line 17 column A less column B plus column C	⊙ 18			10,265.

Job Expenses and Certain Miscellaneous Deductions

19 Unreimbursed employee expenses - job travel, union dues, job education, etc. Attach federal Form 2106 if required. See instructions.............................. ⦿ 19 [   ]

20 Tax preparation fees... ⦿ 20 [   ]

21 Other expenses - investment, safe deposit box, etc. List type ⦿ _____ ⦿ 21 [0.]

22 Add lines 19 through 21... ⦿ 22 [0.]

23 Enter amount from federal Form 1040 or 1040-SR, line 8b ⦿ ____ 6,202.

24 Multiply line 23 by 2% (0.02). If less than zero, enter 0. .... ⦿ 24 [124.]

25 Subtract line 24 from line 22. If line 24 is more than line 22, enter 0. .... ⦿ 25 [0.]

26 **Total Itemized Deductions.** Add line 18 and line 25. .... ⦿ 26 [10,265.]

27 Other adjustments. See instructions. Specify. ⦿ _____ ⦿ 27 [   ]

28 Combine line 26 and line 27. .... ⦿ 28 [10,265.]

29 **Is your federal AGI (Form 540, line 13) more than the amount shown below for your filing status?**

    Single or married/RDP filing separately $200,534
    Head of household $300,805
    Married/RDP filing jointly or qualifying widow(er) $401,072

    No. Transfer the amount on line 28 to line 29.

    Yes. Complete the Itemized Deductions Worksheet in the instructions for Schedule CA (540), line 29 .... ⦿ 29 [10,265.]

30 **Enter the larger of the amount on line 29 or your standard deduction listed below**

    Single or married/RDP filing separately. See instructions............... $4,537
    Married/RDP filing jointly, head of household, or qualifying widow(er) $9,074

    Transfer the amount on line 30 to Form 540, line 18. .... ⦿ 30 [10,265.]

TAXABLE YEAR		FORM
2019	**California Earned Income Tax Credit**	**3514**

Attach to your California Form 540, Form 540 2EZ or Form 540NR

Name(s) as shown on tax return	SSN
HUSSEIN M & SHARISH K ABDULHUSAIN	617755679

Before you begin:

If you claim the EITC even though you know you are not eligible, you may not be allowed to take the credit for up to 10 years.

If you are claiming the California Earned Income Tax Credit (EITC), you must provide your date of birth (DOB), and spouse's/RDP's DOB if filing jointly, on your California Form 540, Form 540 2EZ, or Form 540NR.

If you qualify for the California EITC you may also qualify for the Young Child Tax Credit (YCTC). See instructions for additional information.

Follow Step 1 through Step 9 in the instructions to determine if you meet the requirements, to complete this form, and to figure the amount of the credit(s).

Part I   Qualifying Information   See Specific Instructions.

1 a Has the Internal Revenue Service (IRS) previously disallowed your federal Earned Income Credit (EIC)? ..... ⊙ ☐ Yes ☒ No

b Has the Franchise Tax Board (FTB) previously disallowed your California EITC? .... ⊙ ☐ Yes ☒ No

2 Federal AGI (federal Form 1040 or 1040-SR, line 8b) .... ● 2 | 6202 |.00

3 Federal EIC (federal Form 1040 or 1040-SR, line 18a) .... ● 3 | 2593 |.00

Part II   Investment Income Information

4 Investment Income. See instructions for Step 2 – Investment Income .... ● 4 | |.00

Part III   Qualifying Child Information

You must complete Part I and Part II before filling out Part III. If you are not claiming a qualifying child, skip Part III and go to Step 4 in the instructions.

Qualifying Child Information	Child 1	Child 2	Child 3
5 First name	⊙ AYAAN	⊙	⊙
6 Last name	⊙ ABDULHUSAIN	⊙	⊙
7 SSN	● 891567642	●	●
8 Date of birth (mm/dd/yyyy). If born after 2000 **and** the child is younger than you (or your spouse/RDP, if filing jointly), skip line 9a and line 9b; go to line 10	⊙ 04052019	⊙	⊙
9 a Was the child under age 24 at the end of 2019, a student, and younger than you (or your spouse/RDP, if filing jointly)? If yes, go to line 10. If no, go to line 9b. See instructions	⊙ ☐ Yes ☐ No	⊙ ☐ Yes ☐ No	⊙ ☐ Yes ☐ No
b Was the child permanently and totally disabled during any part of 2019? If yes, go to line 10. If no, stop here. The child is not a qualifying child.	⊙ ☐ Yes ☐ No	⊙ ☐ Yes ☐ No	⊙ ☐ Yes ☐ No
10 Child's relationship to you. See instructions	⊙ SON	⊙	⊙
11 Number of days child lived with you in California during 2019. Do not enter more than 365 days. See instructions	⊙ 365	⊙	⊙

	Child 1	Child 2	Child 3
12 a Child's physical address during 2019 (number, street, and apt. no./sta. no.). See instructions....	⊙ 2447 W ORANGE AVE	⊙	⊙
b City...................	⊙ ANAHEIM	⊙	⊙
c State.................	⊙ CA	⊙	⊙
d ZIP code.............	⊙ 92804-3447	⊙	⊙

Part IV California Earned Income

13 Wages, salaries, tips, and other employee compensation, subject to California withholding. See instructions. ... ● 13 | 2101 |.00

14 IHSS payments. See instructions. .... ⊙ 14 | |.00

15 Prison inmate wages and/or pension or annuity from a nonqualified deferred compensation plan or a nongovernmental IRC Section 457 plan. See instructions. .... ⊙ 15 | |.00

16 Subtract line 14 and line 15 from line 13. .... ● 16 | 2101 |.00

17 Nontaxable combat pay. See instructions. .... ⊙ 17 | |.00

18 Business income or (loss). Enter amount from Worksheet 3, line 5. See instructions. .... ⊙ 18 | 5524 |.00

   a Business name.............. ⊙ UBER AND LYFT

   b Business address.............. ⊙ 2447 W ORANGE AVE

     City, state, and ZIP code........ ⊙ ANAHEIM CA 928043447

   c Business license number .... ⊙

   d SEIN.................... ⊙

   e Business code .... ⊙ 485300

19 California Earned Income. Add line 16, line 17, and line 18. .... ● 19 | 7625 |.00

Part V California Earned Income Tax Credit (Complete Step 6 in the instructions.)

20 California EITC. Enter amount from California Earned Income Tax Credit Worksheet, Part III, line 6. This amount should also be entered on Form 540, line 75; or Form 540 2EZ, line 23. .... ● 20 | 1012 |.00

Part VI   Nonresident or Part-Year Resident California Earned Income Tax Credit

21 CA Exemption Credit Percentage from Form 540NR, line 38. See instructions. . . . ⊙ 21 [   ]

22 **Nonresident or Part-Year Resident EITC.** Multiply line 20 by line 21.
This amount should also be entered on Form 540NR, line 85. . . . . ● 22 [   ] . 00

Part VII   Young Child Tax Credit (YCTC) (See Step 8 in the instructions before completing this part.)

23 **California Earned Income.** Enter the amount from form FTB 3514, line 19. ⊙ 23 [7625] . 00

24 **Available Young Child Tax Credit.** . . . . 24 [1,000] . 00
   • If the amount on line 23 is $25,000 or less, also enter $1,000 on line 28 and skip lines
     25 through 27. If applicable, complete lines 29 and 30.
   • If the amount on line 23 is greater than $25,000, complete lines 25 through 28. If applicable,
     complete lines 29 and 30.

25 **Excess Earned Income over threshold.** Subtract $25,000 from line 23 . . . . ● 25 [   ] . 00

26 Divide line 25 by 100. Enter the result as a decimal out to two decimal places, **do not** round. . . . . ⊙ 26 [   ]

27 **Reduction amount.** Multiply line 26 by $20. Enter the result as a decimal out to two decimal places,
do not round. . . . . ● 27 [   ]

28 **Young Child Tax Credit.**
   • If you did not need to complete lines 25 through 27, your credit is the $1,000 from line 24.
   • If you completed lines 25 through 27, to compute your credit, subtract line 27 from line 24. If your credit
     amount is between $0 and $1, enter $1. If your credit amount is over $1, round to the nearest whole dollar.
This amount should also be entered on Form 540, line 76; or Form 540 2EZ, line 24. . . . . ● 28 [1000] . 00

Part VIII   Nonresident or Part-Year Resident Young Child Tax Credit (See Step 9 in the instructions.)

29 CA Exemption Credit Percentage from Form 540NR, line 38. See instructions . . . . ⊙ 29 [   ]

30 **Nonresident or Part-Year Resident YCTC.** Multiply line 29 by line 28.
This amount should also be entered on Form 540NR, line 86. . . . . ● 30 [   ] . 00

SCHEDULE A
(Form 1040 or 1040-SR)
(Rev. January 2020)
Department of the Treasury
Internal Revenue Service (99)

Itemized Deductions

▶ Go to *www.irs.gov/ScheduleA* for instructions and the latest information.
▶ Attach to Form 1040 or 1040-SR.

Caution: If you are claiming a net qualified disaster loss on Form 4684, see the instructions for line 16.

OMB No. 1545-0074

2019

Attachment
Sequence No. 07

Name(s) shown on Form 1040 or 1040-SR | Your social security number
HUSSEIN M & SHARISH K ABDULHUSAIN | 617-75-5679

Medical and Dental Expenses		**Caution:** Do not include expenses reimbursed or paid by others.			
	1	Medical and dental expenses (see instructions)	**1**	10,530.	
	2	Enter amount from Form 1040 or 1040-SR, line 8b **2** 6,202.			
	3	Multiply line 2 by 7.5% (0.075)	**3**	465.	
	4	Subtract line 3 from line 1. If line 3 is more than line 1, enter -0-		**4**	10,065.
Taxes You Paid	5	State and local taxes.			
		a State and local income taxes or general sales taxes. You may include either income taxes or general sales taxes on line 5a, but not both. If you elect to include general sales taxes instead of income taxes, check this box ▶ ☐	**5a**	37.	
		b State and local real estate taxes (see instructions)	**5b**		
		c State and local personal property taxes	**5c**	200.	
		d Add lines 5a through 5c	**5d**	237.	
		e Enter the smaller of line 5d or $10,000 ($5,000 if married filing separately)	**5e**	237.	
	6	Other taxes. List type and amount ▶	**6**		
	7	Add lines 5e and 6		**7**	237.
Interest You Paid	8	Home mortgage interest and points. If you didn't use all of your home mortgage loan(s) to buy, build, or improve your home, see instructions and check this box ▶ ☐			
Caution: Your mortgage interest deduction may be limited (see instructions).		a Home mortgage interest and points reported to you on Form 1098. See instructions if limited	**8a**		
		b Home mortgage interest not reported to you on Form 1098. See instructions if limited. If paid to the person from whom you bought the home, see instructions and show that person's name, identifying no., and address ▶	**8b**		
		c Points not reported to you on Form 1098. See instructions for special rules	**8c**		
		d Mortgage insurance premiums (see instructions)	**8d**		
		e Add lines 8a through 8d	**8e**		
	9	Investment interest. Attach Form 4952 if required. See instructions .	**9**		
	10	Add lines 8e and 9		**10**	
Gifts to Charity	11	Gifts by cash or check. If you made any gift of $250 or more, see instructions	**11**		
Caution: If you made a gift and got a benefit for it, see instructions.	12	Other than by cash or check. If you made any gift of $250 or more, see instructions. You **must** attach Form 8283 if over $500.	**12**		
	13	Carryover from prior year	**13**		
	14	Add lines 11 through 13		**14**	
Casualty and Theft Losses	15	Casualty and theft loss(es) from a federally declared disaster (other than net qualified disaster losses). Attach Form 4684 and enter the amount from line 18 of that form. See instructions		**15**	
Other Itemized Deductions	16	Other—from list in instructions. List type and amount ▶		**16**	
Total Itemized Deductions	17	Add the amounts in the far right column for lines 4 through 16. Also, enter this amount on Form 1040 or 1040-SR, line 9		**17**	10,302.
	18	If you elect to itemize deductions even though they are less than your standard deduction, check this box ▶ ☐			

For Paperwork Reduction Act Notice, see the Instructions for Forms 1040 and 1040-SR. 175   Schedule A (Form 1040 or 1040-SR) 2019

ABOUT THE AUTHOR

Brian D. Lerner is an Immigration Lawyer and runs a National Immigration Law Firm for nearly 30 years. He is an attorney who is a certified specialist that might help in Immigration & Nationality Law as issued by the California State Bar, Board of Legal Specialization. Attorney Lerner is an expert in Immigration Law, Removal and Deportation, Citizenship, Waiver and Appeals.

He has been a licensed attorney since 1992 and started the Law Offices of Brian D. Lerner, APC. The immigration practice consists of Immigration and Nationality Law, and everything involved with and regarding immigration which includes citizenship, investment visas, family and employment visas, removal and deportation hearings, appeals, waivers, adjustment, consulate processing and all types of immigration and citizenship matters.

He has represented clients from all over the U.S. and in many countries around the world. One side of his practice is dedicated to keeping people in the U.S. and fighting for their immigration rights, while another side is to get people back who have been deported and removed from the U.S.

Also, there is the affirmative part of Immigration Law which Brian Lerner has helped numerous people come into the U.S. on business visas, investment visas, student visas, fiancée and marriage visas, religious visas and many more. Attorney Lerner has helped immigrants who are victims of crime and domestic violence or ones that are married to abusers.

In other words, Attorney Lerner has a firm that helps people all over the U.S. He has dedicated significant time to preparing numerous petitions and applications for you to get at a fraction of the price of hiring an attorney. He says it is the next best thing to a real attorney because they are real petitions prepared by an expert.

www.ingramcontent.com/pod-product-compliance
Lightning Source LLC
Chambersburg PA
CBHW051757200326
41597CB00025B/4589